H Sellack

LONG BEACH and

RE-3-9278

THE
TWELVE

THE TWELVE

THE STORY OF CHRIST'S APOSTLES

By EDGAR J. GOODSPEED

THE JOHN C. WINSTON COMPANY
Philadelphia · Toronto

In Abiding Memory of

ELFLEDA

1880-1949

ACKNOWLEDGMENTS

The Bible: An American Translation, by J. M. Powis Smith and Edgar J. Goodspeed. Copyright 1939 by The University of Chicago. All quotations from this book are reprinted by permission of The University of Chicago Press.

PREFACE

THE INVITATION to write a book which might do for the twelve apostles what I had sought to do for the Apostle Paul a few years ago at first staggered me; we have so little factual material about them. Yet, on reflection, I felt that they presented a very real and positive appeal to the historian, if not to the biographer. None of them found quite such a faithful and devoted historian as Luke the Physician, but the earliest Gospels have something to tell about most of them, and what they accomplished in the ancient world amounted to a great deal. In three short centuries their message had mastered the Roman Empire, and other powers like Armenia as well. While what we can learn about most of them is disappointingly little, what afterdays made out of them is significant and important. I have therefore thought it worth-while to include much that was done and written in their names by a loyal and devout posterity, seeking diligently to perpetuate their message.

Edgar J. Goodspeed

CONTENTS

PART ONE
The Apostolic Age

I

THE FIRST DISCIPLES

THE FIRST ACT of Jesus' ministry as far as we know was to go to the shore of the Sea of Galilee and call to four fishermen out in their boats in the lake, to join him and become, as he put it, fishers for men. He had presumably walked there from Nazareth, six or eight hours' tramp distant, so it was probably well on in the afternoon when he found them. They promptly and wholeheartedly responded; they had evidently known him and been deeply impressed by him at John's meetings down on the Jordan, where Jesus had been baptized by John and then disappeared into the wilderness to grapple with the great task he saw opening before him. He came back from it many days later to find that John's work had been suppressed and John put in prison by Herod Antipas. This meant that his own hour had come; he began at once to proclaim the presence of the reign of God on earth. He would be the founder of the Kingdom. His old friends of John's camp-meeting days should be his helpers, and he seeks them out and calls them to join him, which they gladly do.

It was not until Jesus' first clashes with the Pharisees over the forgiveness of sins, eating with tax collectors, and curing the sick on the Sabbath, that they called the attention of Herod's people to his activities, and Jesus realized that the

3

same sinister forces that had stopped John were hovering about him. He and his disciples cross the lake in Peter's boat to its eastern shore, and there a great crowd gathers to see and hear him. Almost smothered by the multitude, he leads his closest followers up the hill and there chooses the Twelve —the little group of his intimates and confidants. For he remembers Isaiah, and his great ministry, which ended in martyrdom, and yet was so nobly fruitful through the work of his disciples. They could not save Isaiah, but they had written down his prophecies and preserved them for mankind. Little is said of this in the Gospels, only because the same course had been so immensely fruitful for Jesus' cause that what had happened in Isaiah's case seemed trifling in comparison.

Not that Jesus contemplated the writing of books by his disciples, but he did intend their fellowship to carry on his message, if he had to go the way Isaiah had gone. This strain runs through the Gospel story, to its culmination in the Last Supper, which he so definitely makes his memorial. So the choosing of the Twelve is not only to provide associates and assistants in his preaching, but also to seal his teaching in the hearts of his disciples, Isa. 8:16. For already in the third chapter of Mark, the shadow of the cross falls across the page: the Pharisees consulted with the Herodians about Jesus (3:6), with a view to putting him to death.

Of this chosen band the four Capernaum fishermen are the nucleus, Peter, Andrew, James and John. The other eight Jesus added to the group when his danger was brought home to him by the news of the Pharisees' appeal to the agents of Antipas. How nobly and effectively these twelve ordinary Galileans, with one notable exception, carried out Jesus' hopes and wishes in the face of a hostile world!

2

THE TWELVE APOSTLES

⌐〜⌐

Who were the twelve apostles—Jesus' emissaries whom he chose to be with him, and to go out with his message over a wider territory than he could personally cover? Mark, who doubtless recorded what he had heard from Peter, gives the following list, 3:16-19, informally connected by a series of "ands." "These," he wrote, "were the twelve he appointed:

Peter, which was the name he gave to Simon,
and James the son of Zebedee,
and John, James's brother
(he named them Boanerges, that is, Sons of Thunder),
and Andrew,
and Philip,
and Bartholomew,
and Matthew,
and Thomas,
and James the son of Alpheus,
and Thaddeus,
and Simon the Zealot,
and Judas Iscariot, who betrayed him."

Matthew, however, groups them in pairs, supposedly as

Jesus sent them out, 10:1-4; he emphasizes Peter's leadership
by calling him "first":

"First, Simon, who was called Peter, and his brother Andrew,
    and James the son of Zebedee and his brother John,
             Philip and Bartholomew,
         Thomas and Matthew the tax-collector,
      James the son of Alpheus and Thaddeus,
      Simon the Zealot and Judas Iscariot
           who afterward betrayed him."

We may reasonably suppose that they were all Galileans;
indeed, Luke expressly indicates that, by the exclamation of
the Pentecost pilgrims at Jerusalem, Acts 2:7:
    "'Are not all these men who are speaking Galileans?'"
We must conclude that these were the very pairs in which
Jesus sent them out to extend and establish his work of
announcing the arrival of the Kingdom of God which he was
founding, for it was as its founder that he regarded himself:
Simon and Andrew, James and John, Philip and Bartholomew, Thomas and Matthew, James the son of Alpheus and
Thaddeus, Simon the Zealot and Judas Iscariot.
    Their names are all thoroughly Jewish except Andrew and
Philip, who may have had Jewish names besides the Greek
ones. It has been recently pointed out that we are not to
suppose Jesus' preaching and that of the Twelve on this
journey and afterward produced no fruits among his people
except what is reported in the Acts; Christianity was spread-
ing in lands and ways of which we have no reports in the
New Testament. How, for example, did it reach Rome, well
before A.D. 56, when Paul wrote the Roman Christians a
letter? No, the seed he and the Twelve sowed fell into many
honest and understanding hearts and bore fruit, just as he
knew and said it would. It had reached Damascus, no one

knows how, before Saul was sent there. As Enslin has
recently pointed out, Jesus' message had found fertile soil
and acceptance far beyond the claims of the New Testament
narratives. Of the effectiveness of the apostles and their
preaching not a tithe is reported in the Gospels and the Acts.
This is not mere wishful thinking; it is the unavoidable fact.
Luke has made so much of Paul in the Acts that we almost
come to think he stood alone as a missionary, but there were
other if lesser men and women who had seen the light and
were bearing witness.

We must place side by side with these lists in Matthew
and Mark, a third list supplied by Luke in his Gospel, 6:14-
16: it is instructive to compare it with these earlier ones:

MATTHEW	MARK	LUKE
First, Simon, who was called Peter,	Peter, which was the name he gave to Simon,	Simon, whom he named Peter,
and his brother Andrew,		and his brother Andrew,
and James the son of Zebedee	and James the son of Zebedee,	and James
and his brother John,	and John, James's brother (he named them Boanerges, that is, Sons of Thunder), and Andrew	and John
Philip and Bartholomew,	and Philip and Bartholomew,	and Philip and Bartholomew
Thomas and Matthew the tax-collector,	and Matthew, and Thomas,	and Matthew, and Thomas,
James the son of Alpheus	and James the son of Alpheus,	and James the son of Alpheus
and Thaddeus,	and Thaddeus,	
Simon the Zealot	and Simon the Zealot,	and Simon, who was called the Zealot, and Judas, the son of James,
and Judas Iscariot who afterward betrayed him.	and Judas Iscariot, who betrayed him.	and Judas Iscariot, who turned out a traitor.

Luke's list is repeated in Acts 1:13, but not in the order given in Luke's Gospel, 6:14-16. The order in the Acts is:

Peter and John and James and Andrew,
Philip and Thomas,
Bartholomew and Matthew,
James, the son of Alpheus,
and Simon the Zealot,
and Judas, the son of James.

To this list Matthias is added by the brothers, in the place of Judas Iscariot, the betrayer. The Eleven here appear in a new order, not exactly that of Mark or even of Luke himself in his Gospel. It is clear there was no fixed, uniform order for them.

It is of interest to observe that while the little church added a new twelfth apostle to replace Judas, the man who really took his place in the apostolic leadership was Jesus' brother James, who now came to Jerusalem. As far as he was able he took up Jesus' work, like an apostle, and was so accepted, becoming as Paul called him a pillar of the Jerusalem church, and at times clearly taking the lead of it, Gal. 1:19; 2:9.

The lists may be compactly shown as follows; the order is that of Mark:

(MATT. 10)	(MARK 3)	(LUKE 6)	(Acts 1)
Simon	Simon	Simon	
called Peter	called Peter	named Peter	Peter
Andrew his brother		Andrew his brother	
James son of Zebedee	James son of Zebedee	James	John
John his brother	John, brother of James	John	James
	Andrew		Andrew

Philip	Philip	Philip	Philip
			Thomas
Bartholomew	Bartholomew	Bartholomew	Bartholomew
Thomas			
Matthew	Matthew	Matthew	Matthew
	Thomas	Thomas	
James son of	James son of	James son of	James son of
Alpheus	Alpheus	Alpheus	Alpheus
Thaddeus	Thaddeus		
Simon the Zealot	Simon the Zealot	Simon the Zealot	Simon the Zealot
		Judas son of	Judas son of James
		James	
Judas Iscariot	Judas Iscariot	Judas Iscariot	

The agreement of these two lists, Mark and Luke, is almost complete, if we understand Thaddeus to be identical with Judas the son of James, Luke 6:16. His name naturally calls for fuller identification.

The disappearance of Judas Iscariot from the group led the remaining eleven and the Jerusalem believers to fill his place, casting lots in the old Jewish (and pagan) way between the two men between whom they could not decide, Joseph Barsabbas, known as Justus, and Matthias, and the lot fell on Matthias, Acts 1:26. This name, however, does not reappear in the New Testament, the Apostolic Fathers, or the early apologists. The casting of lots in making an impartial selection was a familiar Jewish practice, appearing in no less than ten of the books of the Old Testament, though oftener as a pagan practice than a Jewish.

Whether the apostles continued to work in pairs, as they clearly did on their first mission, Mark 6:7, is a matter to be dealt with as we consider their subsequent labors. Certainly that was their original way of working. We must only note that the four Galilean fishing partners, whom Jesus called first of all, seem to be mentioned together, as Peter, James, John and Andrew, and the first three continue to be named in that way as forming a little inner circle within the Twelve

at the Transfiguration, Mark 9:2, and the Agony in Gethsemane, Mark 14:33. Nor does Andrew recover his prominence as the partner of Peter as the narrative goes on. He is
named but once in Acts as in Luke. But in the Gospel of
John he is mentioned five times. We shall see that in the
later literature of the apostles, Andrew actively reappears as
the missionary to Greece and Macedonia until his martyrdom
at Patras.

This act of Jesus in calling together a definite band of
disciples to be his pupils and emissaries recalls the course
taken in Judah by the Prophet Isaiah seven centuries before,
for he too had an inner circle of men devoted to him and his
work, to whom he seems to have bequeathed his teaching,
for its preservation until better days. Isaiah had gone the
way of martyrdom, but he had bound up his testimony and
sealed his teaching in the hearts of his disciples, Isa. 8:16,
and how gloriously it had survived! We owe the existence
of the Book of Isaiah to those disciples who had made it their
business to record so much that the prophet had said until
the persecution was past, and the book recording his work
and embodying his teaching could be made known. Jesus
certainly knew it well. How often and how tellingly he
quoted Isaiah!

While most of Jesus' apostles seem to do very little of note
during his brief ministry, at least three of them did great
service to his cause after his departure, and we may well
suppose that all of them but one served his church loyally
in its earliest years. We must not fall into the error of thinking the Acts of the Apostles tells more than a very small
fraction of the spread of Jesus' influence; Paul alone, and he
not one of the Twelve, found a historian. Certainly we may
well believe that the Eleven became the nucleus of the
Christian Church.

Yet we have no business to assume that Jesus' own

preaching was of no effect; indeed, nothing could be more unlikely. For some months he had been going about Galilee and then Trans-Jordan, preaching almost constantly, and he was confident some of this seed fell into good and honest hearts and would bear fruit. We must not suppose that the twelve apostles were his only devoted followers at the time of his Crucifixion, or even that the fruits, direct or indirect, of his personal preaching were confined to Palestine. There was a good deal of travel, of moving about from place to place, going on in the Roman world of the first century, and Jesus' teaching was certainly news; he called it that himself, Mark 1:15.

It is necessary to say these things because we are haunted with the mistaken idea that anything not recorded in the New Testament did not happen; that it tells the whole story of the impact of the gospel upon the ancient world, or that Paul did all the missionary work that was done. The seven churches of Asia are enough to correct that idea, Revelation, chapters 1 to 3.

Jesus' purpose in calling the twelve disciples to be his apostles is very plainly stated in Mark: "He appointed twelve of them, whom he called apostles, to be with him and to be sent out to preach," 3:14. He proposed to teach them more fully than he could the shifting multitudes, and thus to perpetuate his teaching, whatever might happen to him. Isaiah's procedure and fate were before him, as he indicated more than once. He would send the Twelve on his errands and their missions, and thus extend the sway of the Kingdom of God he was seeking to set up in the world, and he would have their company and support in times of stress or exaltation; he took three of them with him into the Transfiguration experience. His anxiety to have them with him at the Last Supper and in his anguish of spirit later in the Garden illustrate this.

It is noteworthy that none of Jesus' brothers was included, but the reason is very clear; they did not look upon his great ideas and lofty aims with sympathy and understanding. Indeed, they made determined efforts to deter him from his work and even came with his mother from Nazareth up to Capernaum, to Peter's house, to persuade him to give it up. It was only after it was over that the eldest of them moved to Jerusalem and put himself at the head of the church there— James the Lord's brother, Paul calls him, and he became one of the pillars of the Jerusalem church: "James, Cephas, and John, who were regarded as pillars of the church," Gal. 2:9— and seems to have been recognized as virtually an apostle, if not the chief of them!

It is sad to say that in Jesus' moment of extreme peril the disciples all forsook him and fled, Matt. 26:56. But they could only have perished with him, and so defeated the survival of his work, as Isaiah's disciples had made his work survive his martyrdom. Eventually at least two of the Twelve suffered martyrdom, Peter and James. Tradition, if it is to be believed, made martyrs of others of them—Andrew, Matthew, Thomas.

The boat so often mentioned in the story as the scene of the action has a certain interest for us in the earliest narratives. How it is today I do not know, but years ago a typical fishing boat on Galilee was perhaps 22 feet long and some 8 feet wide. Five boatmen propelled it with short oars in rope loops; I took an oar myself for a while; I wanted to "feel" the water of Galilee. There were four of us in our party, and there was room for two or three more. It was no doubt very much such a boat as Simon's back in the first century, quite capable of holding Jesus and the Twelve, as Mark records.

In such a boat Jesus and his growing band of close associates—his disciples—almost lived, for some months, as he passed from one side of the lake to the other; it was easily crossed in two or three hours, with sail and oars. In this task Andrew, of course, was Peter's principal aide.

As we look at these closest disciples of Jesus, his actual apostles—his messengers and delegates—the one of them most likely to have been capable of writing a Gospel is obviously Matthew, the man of records and figures who knows something at least about putting things down! Yet the Gospel we know by the name of Matthew owes most of its narrative unmistakably to the Gospel of Mark! Or is it possible that the writer of the Gospel of Matthew, while he relied upon Mark so largely, was able to add from other sources, perhaps aided by his own memories, the great teaching sections which give Matthew its distinction and, from the point of view of Jesus' teaching, its supremacy?

3

THE APOSTOLIC PAIRS

M ATTHEW ALONE of the Evangelists scrupulously lists the apostles in pairs, supposedly as Jesus sent them out, two by two, on their first mission, Matt. 10:2-4.

Peter and Andrew

Andrew is paired with Peter in the early scene in the Gospel of Mark when Jesus calls the two brothers to be his followers. Andrew (Andreas) is a Greek name; no Jewish name for him is given. No doubt Andrew as well as Peter had been at John's meetings at the Jordan some weeks before; Jesus' acquaintance with them and their immediate obedience to his summons make that plain. Andrew also appears in Mark as joint occupant of Peter's house in Capernaum, Mark 1:29, to which they all again later repair after Jesus' appearance and after his address in the synagogue. At their house they tell him of Peter's mother-in-law, sick with a fever, upstairs, and he goes up and cures her. From this point on, the brothers' house and their boat are taken for granted in the story. When Jesus goes out to a lonely place early next morning for a time of quiet reflection, Peter and the

14

others find him and try to bring him back to meet the gathering crowd.

A few days later the men who came bringing the paralytic could not get in for the crowd and broke up the roof over Jesus' head to lower the paralytic before him! It was certainly Jesus' home by this time. He had just chosen the Twelve when his relatives, his mother and his brothers, came to stop him, thinking him out of his mind, Mark 3:21. The house was full of his listeners, so his mother and his brothers stood outside and sent word in to him to come outside to them. So much at home was he in the house of Simon and Andrew. From it Jesus set out on his short journeys and to it he returned. Their boat was also his for all his journeys about the beautiful lake, and set him on his way in his three departures from the territory of Antipas, when it became clear that Antipas would like to treat him as he had treated John the Baptist. So through fair weather and foul, all that Simon and Andrew had was Jesus' to use as his own. Yet Andrew was not taken with the three who witnessed the Transfiguration, nor was he with the three who accompanied Jesus in the Garden of Gethsemane. He was a devoted disciple, he certainly did all he could, but he evidently did not have the deeper understanding of Jesus which these experiences demanded. Yet singularly enough, the discourse on the Fall of the City and the End of the Age, uttered on the slopes of the Mount of Olives looking across the Kidron to the Temple, was called forth by the questions of the original four disciples, Peter, James, John and Andrew, Mark 13:3, 4.

Twenty years after the appearance of the Gospel of Luke and its companion volume, the Acts of the Apostles, the Gospel of John found a place for Andrew in its account of the ministry of John the Baptist at the Jordan. John records that Andrew was one of two disciples of John the Baptist who heard John point out Jesus as the Lamb of God, the one upon

whom the Spirit had descended at his baptism. They followed
Jesus to his lodging and spent the rest of the day with him,
John 1:39. Andrew hastened to tell Peter that they had found
the long-expected Messiah, and took him to Jesus, who at
once hailed him as Kephas, the Aramaic word for Rock;
Petros is its Greek equivalent. So Peter had three names in
the New Testament, his given name Simon; the name Jesus
gave him, Kepha, written Kephas in Greek, and Cephas in
English, and used by Paul in speaking of him, Gal. 1:18;
2:9, 11, 14; and the Greek translation of it, Petros, in English
Peter. We must note that Jesus addressed him as "son of
John," John 1:42; 21:15, 16, 17. Sometimes in Matthew and
Luke and frequently in John he is called Simon Peter. In the
Letters of Peter he is called Peter in I Peter; Simon (or even
Symeon) Peter in the second letter. No New Testament
figure has such a variety of names applied to him: Simon,
Simon son of John, Cephas, Peter, Simon Peter. Our first
mentions of him in literature are from Paul, four times as
Cephas in Galatians, A.D. 52, and four times in First Corin-
thians, A.D. 53; and as Peter twice in Galatians. Paul seems
to have thought of him usually as Kephas. No doubt they
talked Aramaic when they met; if Peter knew Greek, he knew
Aramaic far better. "Cephas" does not appear in the Acts
or in the Gospels, except in John 1:42.

Andrew is barely mentioned in the Acts of the Apostles,
1:13, and never in the New Testament letters or the Revela-
tion. In the so-called Apostolic Fathers, next most ancient
Christian writings, and in the early Christian apologists—
Justin, Tatian, Athenagoras, etc., he is not mentioned.
Augustine, however, speaks of a Gospel of Andrew, but
nothing is known of such a work, and it is probably a mistake
for the Acts of Andrew, a work written in his name about
A.D. 260, full of his supposed wanderings over Greece and
Macedonia and his innumerable wonders, ending with his

martyrdom at Patras, by crucifixion. This work was intended
to discourage marriage, and persuade women to leave their
husbands. Later legendry made Andrew's cross X-shaped,
and he is supposed to have lingered upon it for three days,
preaching to the spectators. Another book of the Acts of
Andrew even more extravagant was found by Gregory of
Tours in the sixth century, but like the third-century Acts is
quite unhistorical.

We must not suppose that Andrew did not do a useful
missionary work in his obscurity, even though he did not
achieve the renown of his spirited and impulsive brother. As
we have seen, most of the widest missionary work of the
Early Church was done obscurely by persons unknown but
nonetheless deeply devoted to the great cause of Christ.
Indeed, Andrew is one of the five apostles reported by
Armenian tradition as having worked in the evangelization
of Armenia.

James and John

The second pair of apostles, like the first, are brothers, and
fishermen from the neighboring town of Capernaum, which
seems to have adjoined Bethsaida. These men were the sons
of Zebedee, who was with them when Jesus called to them
to follow him. The four fishermen were partners in the fishing
business, and James and John, as we have seen, came to
form with Peter a small inner circle; at any rate, they were
chosen by Jesus to go with him to the Mount of Transfiguration, Mark 9:2-4, and to be nearest him in the Agony in the
Garden, 14:33. But it was the four that came to him, 13:3, as
he was sitting on the Mount of Olives opposite the Temple,
and asked the question that called forth the great discourse
on the destruction of the city and the End of the Age, that
makes up the thirteenth chapter of Mark.

James and John were the ambitious men who on the way
up to Jerusalem, in their perfect confidence in Jesus' success
and acceptance there, asked him for the two chief places in
his triumph. This strikes us as strangely disregarding Peter, to
say the least. Was there to be no high place for him? But
Jesus' reply throws a somber light on the fate of these close
disciples, for it foreshadows their martyrdom.

" 'You shall drink the cup that I am drinking, and you shall
undergo the baptism that I am undergoing.' "

Acts records that Herod Agrippa I (A.D. 41-44) had James
beheaded, so that Jesus' prediction was fulfilled in little more
than a dozen years. James was the first of the Twelve to die
a martyr's death, probably in A.D. 42, Acts 12:2. Of John's
martyrdom we have no record. Efforts to identify him with
the writer of the Revelation (John the Christian prophet of
Ephesus), or of the Gospel of John, or with the beloved
disciple of John 13:23 and 21:20, are unconvincing. The
beloved disciple is an ideal figure, such a follower as would
have understood Jesus as none of the Twelve did. It is with
such an ideal follower that the author of John, chapters 1-20,
is identified, after his death, by his disciples, when they
write the later conclusion of the Gospel of John, chapter 21.
The earlier Gospels, Mark, Matthew, Luke, know of no such
loyal intimate; they all forsook him and fled, Mark 14:50;
Matt. 26:56.

Matthew's account of the strange request of James and
John that they be given the chief places in what they expected to be his coming triumph is softened and yet height-
ened by putting it into the mouth of their mother, who was
probably Salome. Even there she is evidently their spokesman, for they are with her to back up her request! Matt.
20:20-24. Students of the Gospel point out that it is more
likely that Matthew introduced her into Mark's narrative,
which he follows phrase by phrase with hardly an omission,

to spare the disciples, than that some editor of Mark left it out, to spare their mother!

There is no record of such a fate (martyrdom) for John, however; indeed little more is known of him, for the second-century Acts of John, written about A.D. 170-180, seem to be wholly fictitious. That work was about the length of the Gospel of Matthew and was colored by the heretical Docetic and Gnostic views of the second century. But it knows nothing of John's suffering martyrdom and describes him as dying peacefully, surrounded by his disciples.

The mother of James and John was one of the women who followed Jesus and the Twelve to Jerusalem on the final journey. Certainly if on the way she broached this subject, they supported her in it, Matt. 20:22. At any rate, she was among the women who witnessed the Crucifixion, ch. 27:56, where Mark seems to identify her as Salome, Mark 15:40; it is clear that Matthew believed that to be the name of the mother of James and John. Some have even thought, from John's mention of the third woman at the cross as Jesus' mother's sister, ch. 19:25, that Salome was a sister of Mary, but this cannot be described as certain. If it were, it would make James and John the cousins of Jesus, and put a new aspect on their bold request.

Philip and Bartholomew

The third pair of apostles includes Philip and Bartholomew. Philip, like Andrew, has a Greek name. The oldest Gospels have almost nothing to say of him, in fact, he is mentioned only once in each of the Synoptics; Matthew, Mark and Luke simply name him among the Twelve and say nothing further about him. But he has an important role in the first chapter of John, at Bethany across the Jordan, where John was preaching and baptizing, 1:28. Andrew and another of John's disciples were with John when he pointed to Jesus, who was passing by, and declared him to be God's Lamb, meaning of course his sacrificial lamb. Philip seems to have been one of these two to whom John had so strikingly described Jesus. Two days later Jesus sought out Philip, inviting him to accompany him, apparently on his return to Galilee, and Philip brought Nathanael (which some have thought another name for Bartholomew) to meet him.

Further on in John, it is with Philip that Jesus talks about how to feed the five thousand at the Sea of Galilee, 6:5, 7, and again in 12:21, 22, it is through Philip that Greek inquirers for Jesus seek an introduction to him. Again in 14:8, 9 it is Philip who makes the bold request,

" 'Master, let us see the Father, and it will satisfy us.' "

It will be seen that Philip is given a much larger part in John than in the earlier Gospels, but we must recognize that John's purpose is less historical than theirs was.

Two further Christian leaders named Philip appear in the Acts, where Philip is listed with the eleven apostles, to whom Matthias is now added, to take the place of Judas, 1:26. The appointment of seven deacons, primarily to look after practical sides of church life, 6:5, had a Philip in second place, after Stephen, and his work with the Ethiopian pilgrim, 8:26-40, is still regarded among Ethiopian Christians as the virtual founding of their church. Another Philip was Philip the Missionary, or Evangelist, of Caesarea, whose four daughters had the gift of prophecy, that is, of inspiration in preaching, and who entertained Paul and his companions on their way to Jerusalem for the last time, Acts 21:8, 9. But these men, the deacon and the missionary, are not to be confused with Philip the Apostle.

The name of Philip's companion Bartholomew, in the mission of the Twelve to the Jewish people of Galilee and the adjacent region, has a thoroughly Jewish meaning, "the Son of Tolmai." But it had probably lost that sense and become an individual name. While it duly appears in all the lists of apostles, the New Testament has nothing more to tell us about Bartholomew, and we must gather what we can about him from subsequent Christian literature. We are struck by the fact that in the Acts list of the apostles who reassembled to resume the work of the Kingdom, Bartholomew is paired not with Philip, as in the Gospels, but with Matthew.

While the books of the New Testament make no further mention of Bartholomew, beyond these four mentions in the lists in Matthew, Mark, Luke and Acts, and the earliest subsequent Christian writings give us no definite information about his work or his fate, Eusebius, in his *Church History,* written about A.D. 326, quoting from Pantaenus of Alexandria (about A.D. 150), states that he carried the gospel to India, possibly meaning the Bosporus region, for in that day India had a much wider meaning than now, including Arabia Felix and reaching almost to the borders of Palestine.

There, Pantaenus reported, he found the Gospel of Matthew in Hebrew, meaning Aramaic (cf. Acts 21:40; 22:2; 26:14), which was hardly possible, as it was not written until well after the Jewish War with Rome, or about A.D. 80. Moreover, Matthew's close resemblance to Mark in Greek phraseology as well as incident makes such a document most improbable, unless as a translation from the Greek, in which case Aramaic must be meant.

Under the influence of an Armenian girl at Stanford University, the Armenian church has undertaken the translation of the Bible into modern spoken Armenian. Her name is Louise Nalbandian. The church does this with all devotion to Thaddeus and Bartholomew, who according to Armenian tradition first brought the gospel to Armenia. Certainly in just such ways the gospel found its way not only into the Greek world to which Paul introduced it, but into all the

adjacent regions. Syria even claimed a written correspondence between Jesus and Abgar, king of Edessa, A.D. 13-50.
Abgar opened the alleged correspondence as follows:

> Abgar, ruler of Edessa, to Jesus the excellent Savior, who has
> appeared in the country of Jerusalem, greeting. I have heard the
> reports of you and of your cures as performed by you without
> medicines or herbs. For it is said that you make the blind see and
> the lame walk, that you cleanse lepers and cast out foul spirits
> and demons, and that you heal those afflicted with lingering
> disease, and raise the dead. And having heard all these things
> about you I have concluded that one of two things must be true;
> either you are God, and having come down from heaven you do
> these things, or else you who do these things are the Son of God.
> I have therefore written to you to ask you to take the trouble
> to come to me and heal the disease I have. For I have heard that
> the Jews are murmuring against you, and are plotting to injure
> you. But I have a very small yet noble city which is large enough
> for us both.

To this quaint letter, the Syrian story continues, Jesus
replied:

> Blessed are you who have believed in me without having seen
> me. For it is written that those who have seen me will not be-
> lieve in me, and those who have not seen me will believe and be
> saved. But in regard to what you have written me, that I should
> come to you, it is necessary for me to fulfil all things here for
> which I was sent, and after I have fulfilled them thus to be taken
> up again to him that sent me. But after I have been taken up I
> will send to you one of my disciples to heal your disease and give
> life to you and yours.

In historical fact, Syrian Christianity did not really begin
until about A.D. 172, with Tatian, who united the four
Gospels into one continuous narrative, translating it all into

Syriac for the purpose of evangelizing the Syriac-speaking Syrians. It did not reach the stage of church consciousness reflected in the Abgar correspondence until the middle of the third century, when it was probably written. Eusebius seems to have found the two quaint letters in Syriac in Edessa, and put them into Greek for his *Church History*. They are found in Book 1, Chapter 13. They were soon enriched with the further story that Abgar's messenger painted a portrait of Jesus and took it back to Abgar at Edessa. In a fuller form, the *Teaching of Addai*, the letters passed into Armenian and Greek. The story became widely known through Eusebius' statement and the Latin version of it by Rufinus. The text of Jesus' letter has been found in an inscription in a cave at Edessa, and both letters in a Philippi inscription. Indeed, it became necessary for Pope Gelasius I, A.D. 492-496, to denounce them as apocryphal in his famous decree, now assigned to the sixth century.

Quite apart from this spurious correspondence, the gospel found its way very early even in apostolic times into Syria, where it came first through Aramaic-speaking Christians, and very quickly as the Acts records, began to reach Greeks as well, Acts 11:20-26. As Aramaic and Syriac are closely related languages, it must have reached Syriac-speaking Syrians very early.

The Ethiopians of today trace the existence of Christianity among them back to the Ethiopian eunuch, converted by Philip the Deacon, as reported in Acts 8:27-40.

It is very doubtful whether Christianity really maintained itself in Ethiopia from apostolic times on, as the Ethiopians think; its literature is not notably primitive as Christian literatures go, though it has fragments of the Acts of Paul as we shall see. Its New Testament, however, is of extraordinary interest, being the longest of all forms of the New Testament, as the Syriac was the shortest. The Syriac contained only twenty-two books, instead of the usual twenty-seven we know; it lacked the Revelation and four of the catholic or general epistles—Second Peter, Second and Third John and Jude. But the Ethiopic added to our twenty-seven the so-called *"Clement"* and the *Synodus*. "Clement" consists of a mass of the Clementine literature known to us already, but imbedded in this, modern research has revealed the whole text of the *Revelation of Peter*, A.D. 125-150. The *Synodus* which concluded the book had to do with the "coming together" of the Christian body, and the service then to be followed, a good deal as a prayer book does in a modern liturgical church. But the presence of the *Revelation of Peter*, which had completely disappeared from Mediterranean Christianity some sixteen hundred years ago, shows the extreme antiquity of the contents of the Ethiopic New Testament and its independence of Mediterranean influence through that length of time.

Whatever became of those we may call the minor apostles, at least the less celebrated ones, has been a tempting subject of imagination beginning with the second century. The field of fiction was being explored by the Greek writers of the day and Christian writers did not escape its attraction. Besides, if there had to be fiction, they may have thought, let us have our own Christian fiction, for Christian readers—a religious fiction that shall not degrade and defile its readers, but edify and improve them. So we must explain the wealth of these unhistorical acts and gospels which we shall find sprang up in the second and third centuries.

Thomas and Matthew

This is the order in which the Gospel of Matthew names the fourth pair of apostles, though Mark and Luke's Gospels put Matthew first, and the list in Acts pairs Thomas with

Philip—"Philip and Thomas." Only in John, where Thomas is three times mentioned, 11:16; 20:24; 21:2, is the phrase "who was called the Twin" added. The procedure of the earlier translators, beginning with the Latin Vulgate version of Jerome, made in A.D. 380-400, was to take the somewhat unusual word Didymus as a proper name. This course was followed by William Tyndale and the whole historic series of seven English Bibles through King James, to the English Revised Version of 1881 and the American Standard Version of 1901. The word is never found as a proper name in the Greek papyri, and so the translators of the present century have translated it, the Twin, in which the Revised Standard Version of 1946 and 1950 has concurred. We can only suppose that Thomas was one of a pair of twins, though who his twin was we are nowhere told. We are not even certain that it was a proper name; "T'hom" in Hebrew means "Twin." Didymus seems to be a translation of this word into Greek. But in antiquity the first of a pair of twins was named, the second often being simply called "Twin" (Didymus).

The incident of Thomas being absent from the Twelve when they had their convincing experience of the Resurrection led to his doubts, indeed his complete disbelief in their report, and to his becoming the type of incredulity and doubt. He had shown a similar attitude when they were approaching Jerusalem, and he said, with despairing courage, John 11:16,

" 'Let us go also, and die with him!' "

So he becomes in the Gospel of John the representative of the doubting type of mind.

Matthew is one of the few apostles of whose call by Jesus we have a definite account. It is given in the Gospel of Mark, 2:14-17, and taken over into Matthew, 9:9-13, with the change of "Levi, the son of Alpheus" to "a man called Matthew." Matthew's account also adds v. 13a, "You must go and learn what the saying means, 'It is mercy, not sacrifice, that I care for.' " Only the Gospel of Matthew gives the tax-collector apostle this name, in telling the story of his call. Luke like Mark speaks of him here as Levi, 5:27, although both Mark and Luke in their lists of the apostles list nobody named Levi, but read Matthew as seventh in the list, Mark 3:18; Luke 6:15. Yet it is clear that the writer of the Gospel of Matthew is here drawing upon that of Mark, while revising and enriching it.

Jesus saw Matthew sitting at his tax-collecting office, on the shore of the lake, perhaps figuring out the proper tax each fisherman should pay on the fish he brought ashore to market. Jesus called him, saying simply,

"Follow me."

Matthew got right up and followed him, and that afternoon or evening, Luke tells us, entertained Jesus at dinner with many tax collectors and people the scribes considered "sinners," since they did not observe the rabbinical details of the Law.

The Gospel of Matthew, which bears the name of the seventh apostle (the eighth in Matthew, who transposes Thomas and Matthew), was probably written in Antioch in Syria a few years after the Jewish War. It was largely built upon the Gospel of Mark, written in Rome about A.D. 70. I find fully fifteen-sixteenths of Mark reproduced with very little verbal change in the Gospel of Matthew, but Canon Streeter found nineteen-twentieths of Mark reproduced almost word for word in Matthew. Yet Matthew adds so much of Jesus' teaching (like the Sermon on the Mount) that his Gospel has far surpassed Mark's in religious influence and effectiveness ever since!

Was it the tax-collector apostle who penned it? So thought the Early Church, probably by A.D. 125, when it assembled the four Gospels, and gave each its name, and while we cannot confirm it, we cannot deny it either, unless the writer's great dependence upon Mark's wording, page after page, compels it. The writer was entirely at home in the familiar everyday Greek spoken all about the Mediterranean, from Antioch even as far as the old Greek business cities of Gaul and Spain. The purpose of the writer of the Gospel of Matthew is evidently to make the clear and vigorous narrative of Mark carry the amazing and precious religious message of Jesus in all the fulness in which he could provide it, though not even he could exhaust it, as Luke and John were later to show.

Matthew was evidently a man of larger means than most of the apostles, as the dinner he gave when he was called by Jesus to be one of his followers, and indeed his profession as a tax collector, implied. Four of the apostles were fishermen, Zebedee's sons and their partners, Simon and Andrew, making up with their hired helpers quite an organization, as we should say, Mark 1:20; Luke 5:7, 10.

Matthew was probably a man of somewhat more education, as we would call it, than some of his fellow disciples. He must have been able to read and write, and to use the elements at least of arithmetic, in his work as a tax collector, at any level. The numerous Greek papyri from the first and second centuries that have emerged from the sands of Egypt in the past fifty years have given abundant evidence of such practices. One Greek papyrus of A.D. 190, over eight feet in length and written on both sides, preserves over 1,200 items in forty-seven columns of amounts in drachmas received from or paid out to all sorts of people for every sort of purpose. The writer uses his reed pen until it become little better than a stick, when at last he sharpens it, and his handwriting suddenly becomes a fine clear hand! Such men were not rare

about the eastern Mediterranean in New Testament times.
More than one published volume contains pages of tax-col-
lectors' records.

A single Oxford volume of Greek papyri includes documents dated in more than fifty different years of the first
century. So general was a business knowledge of writing
and figuring. Nor did they have to use the clumsy Latin
numbers, so ill adapted to rapid business use. The Greek
letters were also figures, k was 20; l, 30; m, 40; n, 50; r, 100;
s, 200; t, 300, etc.

Certainly a few years after the fearful Jewish War with
its appalling carnage and devastation, a deeply religious
believer at Antioch, where church and synagogue were
already in vigorous conflict and competition, drove home the
lesson of the Jewish War as a judgment upon the Jewish
people for its rejection of its Messiah, but far beyond that,
made his book the greatest vehicle for the message of the
Kingdom of Heaven it is likely ever to get. We cannot surely
say this author was the Apostle Matthew, the ex-tax collector,
and yet no more probable identification occurs to us. We
may remember that the Jews had much less interest in who
wrote a book than the Greeks had or than we have, and the
Christian movement was growing up in what was in many
ways a Jewish atmosphere. Yet Matthew was written in
Greek, and reproduced almost everything in the Greek Mark.

Matthew was at any rate the first of the twelve apostles
credited by the early Christians with having written a
Gospel, though very soon, in the second quarter of the second century, other "apostolic" gospels appeared, partly under
the influence of the last verse in the Gospel of John, which
seems almost to invite such publications: "There are many
other things that Jesus did, so many in fact that if they were
all written out, I do not suppose that the world itself would
hold the books that would have to be written."

Our four Gospels were collected and published together by the year 125; John at least was current in a leaf-book if not from that time, certainly within ten or fifteen years, as the Rylands Library fragment from the time of Hadrian, A.D. 117-138, clearly shows. Gospels of the Hebrews, Peter, and the Egyptians made their appearance by A.D. 140, but made no lasting place for themselves in Christian use, and only fragments of them remain today. As we have seen, the Gospel of Mark is really in substance Peter's great basic contribution to the gospel fabric, even though he made it unconsciously in his preaching at Rome, and it was first written down consecutively after his martyrdom and naturally came to be called by the name of the man who wrote it down.

The Matthias who was added to the list of apostles after the desertion and death of Judas, as reported in the first chapter of Acts, plays no visible part in the subsequent narrative, but he is credited in later Christian tradition with having written a book called the *Traditions of Matthias.* Perhaps Paul's use of the word "traditions" in I Cor. 11:2 and II Thess. 2:15 suggested the use of that title. Clement of Alexandria uses the book and quotes from it, A.D. 190-210, and it was probably written not long before his time, or fully a century after the lifetime of the Apostle Matthias.

Yet it is plain that something toward preserving Jesus' sayings from oblivion had been done by the primitive disciples, and they had to some extent taken definite shape in Christian memory almost at once after his departure. The fortnight Paul had with Peter, Gal. 1:18, must have given Paul direct personal memories of Jesus and his teachings of the utmost interest and value, and we find him later writing to the Corinthians what is our earliest account of the institution of the Lord's Supper, and the words Jesus used of the bread and the wine, I Cor. 11:23-25. These must have been told Paul by Peter, with much besides of Jesus' teachings during that visit. They are not identical in language with his words given in Mark 14:22-25, but they agree in substance, and in order (bread first, then wine), against Luke, who has the cup preceding the bread. In the Passover the fourth cup preceded the taking of the bread, which was then followed by the fifth and final cup (or sip) of wine. Luke understood the fourth cup to be the one Jesus hallowed at the Supper; Paul and Mark, doubtless following Peter's report of the incident, made it the fifth, with which the Lord's Supper, like the Passover before it, concluded. Matthew, of course, followed Mark, Matt. 26:26-29, so that Matthew, Mark and Paul agree in the familiar order.

James the Son of Alpheus, and Thaddeus

This James is also spoken of as James the Less, probably because he was shorter than James the son of Zebedee, but possibly because he was less important. The other James was the first of the apostles to suffer martyrdom, and besides he was one of the inner circle, Peter and James and John. But James, "the Less" as it is sometimes translated, had a distinguished brother, for Levi, better known as Matthew, was also a son of Alpheus, as was Joses, who though not an apostle was close to the circle. His mother Mary was one of the women who witnessed the Crucifixion, Mark 15:40, see also 16:1. We only wish we had more information about the head of this interesting family, Alpheus himself.

Thaddeus, as Judas the son of James is called by Matthew, 10:3 and Mark 3:18, is credited to this day in Armenian tradition with having brought the gospel to Armenia with notable success. Armenia declared itself a Christian people in A.D. 301. Of what James he was the son we are not told.

Simon the Zealot and Judas Iscariot

Paired with Judas in the sending out of the Twelve was Simon the Cananaean, meaning the Zealot. This party arose among the Jews in attempted resistance to the census of Quirinius, in A.D. 6 or 7. They were altogether unreconciled to the domination of Rome and were militant in their devotion to the Messianic hope. A generation later, when the Jews rebelled against Rome, A.D. 66, they were fanatical in their opposition to the Roman armies, and even to some Jewish groups of whom they disapproved. Old Armenian tradition makes Simon one of the apostles who evangelized Armenia.

The fate of Judas seems to have been of little concern to the Eleven. The Gospel of Matthew, however, devotes a few lines to it, 27:3-10, while Luke treats it still more briefly, Acts 1:16-20. Matthew says that Judas was bribed by the Jewish authorities to betray Jesus, possibly expecting Jesus to extricate himself in some superhuman way. At any rate, he was appalled by his conviction, and tried to return to the high priests and elders the thirty silver pieces they had paid him. They refused it, but Judas threw the money down at their feet and went off and hanged himself in remorse. The Evangelist goes on to tell how the high priests gathered up the money, but felt they could not return it to the Temple treasury since it was "blood money." So they bought with it a piece of ground known as the Potter's Field, to be used as a burial ground for strangers. Matthew saw in this act a strange fulfilment of some words he ascribes to Jeremiah, which are not in our Jeremiah, but in Zech. 11:13. Some lines in Jer. 18:2 and 19:1 and 11 about potters and their work may have been in Matthew's mind. Thirty shekels of silver were just the wages of the Foolish Shepherd in Zech. 11:12, 13.

Luke's account of the fate of Judas is quite different. In Acts 1:18, 19 he says that Judas bought a piece of land with the money, and his body swelled up and burst open and all his vitals poured out, in consequence of which the piece of land came to be called the Bloody Field—in Aramaic Akelda-mach. Some see in this strange statement a reflection of the popular story of Ahiqar, in which Nadan the traitor comes to just such an end. In general, the Christian leaders seem to have lost all interest in Judas almost at once; Peter and Paul had nothing to say about him; for them, he simply disappeared without a trace. He had no part in the great sequel.

The seventy-two emissaries—so the oldest manuscripts read—sent out by Jesus in anticipation of his great journey to Jerusalem, Luke 10:1, while slightly reminiscent of the seventy elders in Num. 11:16, is more closely related to the original mission of the Twelve. There were now to be six messengers to every one of the original Twelve, perhaps captained as it were by the somewhat experienced Twelve. The familiar fact of the twelve tribes may doubtless have operated here to some extent; it was in a sense a mission to Israel, and we catch key slogans of it in the cries along the road at the Triumphal Entry:

> Hosanna!
> "God bless him!
> Blessed be he that comes in the Lord's name! . . .
> God bless him from on high!"

The Seventy-two are to go two by two to every village and town to which Jesus intended to come on his way through Trans-Jordan to Jerusalem, to announce his approach and make such preparations as were necessary for his coming.

THE INDIVIDUAL APOSTLES

1. Simon Called Peter

THE FIRST of the apostles, whose name leads all the lists given in the Gospels of Matthew, Mark and Luke, and the book of Acts, is the most dynamic and striking personality of the Twelve. Of the labors and movements of the group, his are by far the best known. We must not, however, fall into the natural mistake of supposing him to have altogether overshadowed the rest in his missionary usefulness. We must again remember that most of the missionary work of the first generation or two was quietly done, personally and often incidentally, by busy men and women who had believed and communicated the gospel to the people they knew or encountered as they went about the ancient world for whatever reason. Only thus can we explain its early appearance in Damascus; that was why Saul was sent there by the high priest; and its presence in Rome, in surprising strength (a huge multitude, Tacitus reports, martyred there by A.D. 64—Ingens multitudo, *Annals*, xv, 44). But by A.D. 56 there was a Christian group there significant enough to call forth Paul's letter to the Romans.

Yet it must be remembered that this striking eminence of Peter among the Twelve may be in part due to the fact that he was himself, very probably unintentionally, the leading source of our information.

As one reads the story of Peter one is struck with the great gap between him and his fellow apostles. He is easily first among them, and there is no second! Peter towers above them all! His brother Andrew plays little part in what goes on. James the son of Zebedee was an early martyr and so cut off in his prime, Mark 10:39; Acts 12:2. This impression given by the Gospels may have been due in part to the very clear fact that Peter was the main source of the story of Jesus and his life with the Twelve, and he remembered best the scenes and talks in which he had been active—the things he had said to Jesus and Jesus had said to him.

All this is not enough to explain why in history (or tradition) Peter so outdistances the other apostles. What is it that has given him this advantage over the rest of the Twelve?

One such thing is the part he played in creating the tradition of Jesus' ministry and Passion that forms the Gospel of Mark. The inclusion of Peter's lamentable denial of Jesus at the very crisis of his trial is enough to prove that Peter is back of the whole story of Mark. That is the unmistakable impression it gives from first to last. The bewildering confusion of the first page of Mark soon gives way, Mark 1:14, to Jesus' coming to Galilee, calling his friends Simon and Andrew to be his followers, taking up his residence at the house of Simon Peter, or as he asked him, making constant use of his boat and of Peter's services as his boatman and chief assistant. It has been truly said that practically the whole action of Mark goes on in the presence of Peter, and we can only conclude that it consists of his memories of Jesus' ministry and Passion; indeed, for anyone else to put in circulation the dreadful story of his denying Jesus three times over is virtually inconceivable. It would be a shameful reflection on a fellow Christian, even if true! Peter alone could tell that story with decency, and told by him its religious effect would have been terrific. Everyone present would be moved to confession and repentance for his own shortcomings.

The probability that Peter was the narrator of these intimate incidents that fill the Gospel of Mark is overwhelming. Not indeed that he wrote that First Gospel, but that he used these incidents and narratives in his preaching. His translators (for he must have preached in Aramaic), who stood beside him and put his sermons sentence by sentence into Greek for his Greek-speaking public, translated these sayings and stories of his so often that they had assumed definite word-forms in their minds and memories. When he was snatched from them and from his preaching, away in the Greek cities of the west, by the most famous of Christian martyrdoms, and the dreadful realization came that they would never hear these matchless memories from his lips again—their closest and indeed their only approach to the preaching and table talk of Jesus—then the men who had been Peter's interpreters and translators in his otherwise unintelligible preaching awoke to the fact that they, or at least one of them, had his mind stored with what Peter had been uttering, and he sat down to record it before it could be forgotten. So arose beyond doubt the First Gospel, known to us as Mark's. This Gospel not only became the basis, model and the chief source of its two later successors, known to us as Matthew and Luke, but ushered in a new and most potent form of religious literature—the most effective type of religious literature ever devised—the Gospel!

The evidence for Peter's subsequent residence in Rome and work there naturally falls in the treatment of his relation to the Gospel of Mark, later in this book.

2. *James the Son of Zebedee*

The second apostle in Mark's list is James the son of
Zebedee. He is listed ahead of Peter's brother Andrew perhaps because he suffered martyrdom in A.D. 42, as Peter also
did years later. It may be Mark's intention to put the two
martyred apostles first. Or he may be moved by the fact that
Peter, James and John formed an inner three within the
Twelve, as their presence at the Transfiguration and in
Gethsemane suggests. James and John, sons of Zebedee and
engaged with him in the fishing business in the Sea of Galilee, lived in Capernaum or its suburb on the lake, Bethsaida,
which means "fishing place." James and John were called by
Jesus to follow him and be his disciples just after he had
summoned Simon and Andrew, their partners, and the four
who had evidently known Jesus before, presumably at John's
camp meeting on the Jordan, joined him at once, becoming
his first disciples. A few weeks later they formed the nucleus
of the twelve apostles, but none of these later apostles seem
to have possessed the intimacy with Jesus enjoyed by this
first group of four disciples. James was one of the group that
witnessed the Transfiguration and that Jesus took with him
into the Garden of Gethsemane the last night of his life.
Some twelve years later, after sharing the leadership of the
Jerusalem church with Peter most of that time, James was
arrested, probably in A.D. 42, and beheaded by Herod
Agrippa I, who had recently become king of Palestine and
ruled it from A.D. 41-44. James and John were the disciples
who on the way up to Jerusalem with Jesus and the Twelve
asked him to promise them the chief places in his expected
triumph, but he only assured them that they would indeed
drink the cup he had to drink, evidently meaning martyrdom. Yet we have no record of the martyrdom of John, who

shared in the leadership of the Jewish mission with Peter for some years longer.

James became the patron saint of Spain (St. Iago), though the narrative of the Acts, chapters 1-12, leaves no room for a Spanish mission on his part. But the cathedral of Santiago de Compostela is a memorial to him, and his bones are said to lie in the crypt of the cathedral, having been taken there after his martyrdom, but lost track of until the ninth century.

3. John the Son of Zebedee

John—the brother of James, the third of the apostles as listed by Mark, who puts Andrew fourth—was the son of Zebedee and probably Salome, who appears on the journey to Jerusalem to ask for the two chief places in Jesus' coming Kingdom for her sons, Matt. 20:20, 21. (She does not appear, however, in Mark.) She was a witness of the Crucifixion, Matt. 27:56.

Jesus called the two young men "Sons of Thunder," Boanerges, Mark 3:17, perhaps because they wished him to call down fire from heaven upon a Samaritan village that refused to admit him because he was going to Jerusalem, Luke 9:53-56, but he rebuked them for suggesting it.

While the fiery brothers deserted him at his arrest, as he probably wished them to do to carry on his work, in after-days no one worked more faithfully. John was Peter's constant companion and ally, Acts 3:1; 4:13, 19; 5:18-42, he acted with the Twelve, 6:2, and accompanied Peter to Samaria, 8:14. He is mentioned in connection with his brother's martyrdom, 12:2, but little more can be gathered from the Acts about John. An earlier document than any of these, Paul's Letter to the Galatians, mentions him, "James, Cephas, and John, who were regarded as pillars of the church,

pledged Barnabas and me their co-operation." This was in
A.D. 52, so that John had evidently taken his brother's place
at Jerusalem; indeed, he had maintained a high place of his
own ever since the Resurrection.

In subsequent literature however, later than Paul's letters
and Mark, Matthew and Luke-Acts, John disappears, being
lost behind the figures of John the Prophet, of the Revelation, and John the Elder, of the Gospel of John, chapter 21,
and the Epistles of John, especially of the first verse of the
second and third letters of John. Here we must carefully
distinguish three Johns, the Apostle, the Prophet of the Revelation, and the Elder of Ephesus. It was the last of these who
wrote the Fourth Gospel.

4. Andrew the Son of John

The fourth of the apostles in Mark's list, and in Luke's list
in Acts 1:13, is Andrew (Greek, *Andreas*) the brother of
Peter. The other lists put Andrew second, pairing him naturally with his brother Peter, Matt. 10:2; Luke 6:14. It is
clear that Mark was influenced by the subsequent grouping
of Peter, James and John as an inner three, more fully in
Jesus' confidence than Andrew seems to have been; though
in Mark 13:3 he is grouped with them in asking Jesus when
the fall of Jerusalem is to happen. Andrew is a Greek, not a
Hebrew name, meaning "manly," and is found occasionally
in the papyri and in Greek history two centuries before
Christ. Andrew and Philip are the distinctly Greek names
among the apostles.

Andrew shares with Peter the distinction of being the first
apostles or indeed disciples called by Jesus to join him. The
fuller account in John connecting all four men with Jesus
at John's camp meeting seeks to give a background for their
evident acquaintance with him, and it is clear that he is no

stranger to them in the Mark-Matthew-Luke account; but John's explanation of Jesus' naming Simon "Cephas" is less convincing than the account in Matt. 16:18.

Like his brother, Simon, afterward called Peter, Andrew was a fisherman, of Capernaum-Bethsaida, lived in the same house with him and used the same boat.

In John 1:36, 41 and 42, John the Baptist points out Jesus to Andrew as the Lamb of God, and Andrew tells Simon and brings him to Jesus, who immediately names him Cephas— meaning Peter, a rock. The Gospel of John also records that Jesus addressed Peter as Simon son of John, when he named him Cephas.

At the feeding of the five thousand, in John 6:8, 9, it is Andrew who says,

" 'There is a boy here who has five barley loaves and a couple of fish, but what is that among so many people?' "

Andrew is reported in the Armenian tradition as having been one of the five apostles who evangelized that country.

In the later apocryphal literature, about A.D. 260, Andrew is said to have preached and done wonders in Macedonia and Greece, where he especially urged wives to forsake their husbands, and finally suffered martyrdom at Patras (Patrae) in consequence, being crucified on an X-shaped cross (*crux decussata*, later called St. Andrew's cross), on which he lingered for three days, preaching to the bystanders until he died. But this document belongs to the third century.

5. Philip

The fifth apostle in Mark's list, 3:18, is Philip. He is paired in Matthew with Bartholomew and presumably was his comrade and partner when Jesus sent them out to preach, though in the Acts, 1:13, he is the partner of Thomas. Like Andrew, he has a Greek name, but that does not imply that he was

Greek. He is not to be confused with other men of that name in the Acts—Philip the Deacon, of Acts 6:5; 8:26-40, usually identified with Philip the Missionary of 21:8, though this is not certain. Yet it may seem that if Philip of Caesarea was one of the original seven deacons, he would have been called that, instead of the Evangelist or Missionary, unless his success as a missionary, chapter 8, had led to that designation. Philip is also mentioned in John 1:43-46 as having been sought out by Jesus and invited to accompany him, making him the third of the later apostles to have known Jesus at John's meetings, sometime before Jesus began to preach. The Fourth Evangelist thus builds up the idea implicit in Mark's narrative, 1:16-20, that Jesus had known at least some of his later disciples when they were attending John the Baptist's meetings. Clearly the Apostle was not the Deacon, though the Deacon may have become the Missionary.

Philip is mentioned only once in Mark, 3:18, in Matthew, 10:3, and in Luke, 6:14. He also appears in the Acts, 1:13, and we have seen what the Gospel of John says of him. Later Christian tradition mentions a Gospel of Philip, written perhaps late in the second century, but as a vehicle for Gnostic ideas. Epiphanius quotes from it a highly Gnostic sentence: "The Lord revealed to me what the soul must say as it goes up into heaven, and how it must answer each of the powers above." As a matter of fact, we know little or nothing about the fifth apostle except his name.

6. Bartholomew

The sixth apostle listed by Mark is Bartholomew. Bartholomew is paired with Philip in Matthew, so that he stands sixth in both lists, as well as in that of Luke, 6:14. In Acts 1:13, however, Thomas is paired with Philip, and Bartholomew with Matthew. These are the only mentions of Bartholomew in the New Testament; he is mentioned only in the four lists of the apostles. Doubtless there was much to be said of him and his labors, but it had not struck the imagination or engaged the interest of the two chief sources of our information, Mark or Luke. Yet it was precisely the quiet patient work of such obscure figures that mainly won the gospel battle in the world of the first century as it does also in the twentieth. Nor does his name appear anywhere in the Apostolic Fathers or the early Christian apologists of the second century—Aristides, Justin, Tatian, Melito, Athenagoras.

Eusebius in his *Church History* (v:10:3) says that Pantaenus in the second century on his mission to "India" found there a Hebrew (meaning Aramaic) form of the Gospel of Matthew, left there by the Apostle Bartholomew, and this remark of his may have led Jerome a century later to have spoken very casually of a Gospel of Bartholomew! But nothing is known of any such work as either suggests.

As for his mission to "India," in the language of that time it was often a way of describing the Bosporus region not far from Palestine, and there Bartholomew may have preached. We may add the Armenians today hold that the gospel was first brought to their country by Thaddeus and Bartholomew, and they are venerated as the founders of the Armenian church. Certainly the western part of Armenia was Christianized by early in the fourth century; indeed Armenia became officially a Christian country in A.D. 301. Simon the Zealot, Andrew and Matthias are also reported to have shared in the Armenian mission.

7. Matthew (Levi)

The seventh and eighth apostles in Mark's list, 3:18, which names them individually, not as pairs, are Matthew and

Thomas. The Gospel of Matthew gives them as Thomas and Matthew the tax collector, 10:3. Matthew is more fully introduced to the reader by the Evangelists than perhaps any other member of the Twelve. He is introduced in Mark 2:13-15, as Levi the son of Alpheus, a tax collector of Capernaum, who gave a dinner in Jesus' honor. Luke in his account of the same event, 5:27-29, also calls him Levi the son of Alpheus, but Matthew in his account, 9:9, 10, speaks of him as Matthew. In the lists of the twelve apostles, however, all three of them call him Matthew. His toll office may have been on the Mediterranean-Damascus road, where it passed the lake at Capernaum.

The Gospel of Matthew, it is true, says nothing about its writer, any more than the Gospel of Mark does. The main objection to accepting it as the work of the Apostle Matthew, the most literate and capable of writing, as far as we know, of the Twelve, is that it makes such abundant use of the Gospel of Mark, absorbing almost every bit of it, when the Apostle Matthew must have known of most of these happenings himself and had his own views of them. Yet on the other side, he may, indeed he must, have felt the tremendous grip of Mark's story and thought that what it needed was building up on the side of Jesus' teaching and preaching. That was where he most supplemented it, though he did freely depart from its arrangement and order. Certainly Mark's book, good as it was, suggested to him or some other Matthew, the better book that could be written. To find such an author within the apostolic circle seems too good to be true; and yet is it any easier to find him outside that circle? Matthew is more likely to have known Greek than any of the rest, for he was a tax collector. He is likely to have been readier with the pen than most, perhaps than any, of the group, and he may even have jotted down for his own use not a few of Jesus' striking sayings, especially after the missionary travels of the Twelve about the Jewish towns, as almost any Greek would have done. The more you think of it, the more likely it seems that Matthew wrote the Gospel that bears his name! He would feel Mark's inadequacy on the side of Jesus' teaching, and seek to remedy it. Let us deal with this more fully when we reach the Apostolic Gospels in Chapter 7.

8. Thomas

The eighth of the apostles in Mark's list, as well as in Matthew's and Luke's, though the sixth in the Acts, is Thomas. Nothing more is said of him in the New Testament except in the Gospel of John, where he appears in chapters 11; 14; 20; 21. He is on the whole a shadowy figure; we hardly know even his name, which is the Hebrew for "Twin," as Didymus, given in John, chapters 11; 20; 21, is the Greek. Neither Thomas (in Hebrew) nor Didymus (the Greek equivalent of it) have been found among proper names of that period.

9. James the Son of Alpheus

The ninth apostle in Mark's list is James the son of Alpheus. He occupies the same position in Matthew, chapter 10; Luke, chapter 6 and Acts, chapter 1. He was an inconspicuous figure, for he was short in stature or perhaps he was just the younger of the two apostles named James, Mark 15:40. His father's name was Alpheus, Matt. 10:3; Luke 6:15; Acts 1:13; his mother's, Mary, Matt. 27:56; Mark 15:40; 16:1; Luke 24:10. Since his father's name was Alpheus, he may have been Matthew's brother, Mark 2:14.

There was another son of Alpheus among Jesus' followers; his name was Joses, Mark 15:40, 47. Their mother Mary was one of the women who witnessed the Crucifixion. So while we don't know just what the attitude of Alpheus to Jesus was, his wife and three sons "of Alpheus" were among his strongest adherents—supposing the Alpheus mentioned in connection with them is one and the same person. It is not improbable that one of his sons did the Christian cause the magnificent service of writing the Gospel of Matthew.

10. Thaddeus

The tenth apostle in Mark's list, 3:18, followed by Matthew, 10:3, is Thaddeus; Luke's lists, however, both have Simon the Zealot in the tenth place, and Judas the son of James in the eleventh place. It would seem that Thaddeus is another name for this mysterious Judas the son of James. Thaddeus is one of the two apostles credited by Armenian tradition with the evangelization of Armenia; they were Thaddeus and Bartholomew.

11. Simon the Zealot

The eleventh apostle in Mark's list, which is followed as usual by Matthew, 10:4, is Simon the Zealot. Luke, as we have seen, has Judas the son of James, doubtless identical with Thaddeus, in the eleventh place, in both his Gospel and the Acts. The Zealots, as we must translate the Aramaic word "Cananaean" of Matthew 10:4; Mark 3:18, were a half-revolutionary party formed in A.D. 6-7 to resist the census ordered by Quirinius; it survived as a nationalistic anti-Roman faction. Armenian tradition claims Simon as one of its evangelizers.

12. Judas Iscariot

The twelfth in all four lists is Judas Iscariot, who revealed Jesus' presence and whereabouts to the agents of the high priests and so brought about his arrest in the Garden of Gethsemane on the Mount of Olives, and his trial and death. Just why he did this is a many-sided problem; perhaps just for the money, but if so he had not expected Jesus to be put to death, for when that happened he gave back the money and killed himself, Matt. 27:1-5. Such was the explanation current in Antioch. Luke, writing in Ephesus some ten years later, reported that Judas had bought a piece of land with the money paid him and then died the hideous death recorded in the Story of Ahiqar as the fate of the traitor Nadan, who swelled up until he burst.

13. Matthias

While the Matthias who was added to the list of apostles after the desertion and death of Judas, as reported in the first chapter of Acts, plays no visible part in the subsequent narrative, he is credited in later Christian tradition with having written a book called *The Traditions of Matthias*. Perhaps Paul's use of the word "traditions" in I Cor. 11:2 and II Thess. 2:15 suggested the use of that title. Clement of Alexandria uses the book and quotes from it, A.D. 190-210, and it was probably written not long before his time, or fully a century after the lifetime of the Apostle Matthias. Yet some primitive Christian probably did collect without writing them down such sayings of Jesus as Paul, and later the letters known as First and Second Clement, occasionally repeat. Matthias is one of five apostles credited by Armenian tradition with evangelizing Armenia.

5

THE RALLYING OF THE APOSTLES

WE ARE REMINDED of Dr. Enslin's observation that much of the missionary work which so swiftly spread the Christian faith over the Roman world was anonymous—the work of obscure individual believers moving about the ancient world on their ordinary activities, but telling of the gospel as they had opportunity. There were also, and perhaps more importantly, those men who went out to other lands expressly to preach the gospel, but who had no gifts as writers and found no historian. With their expectation of an early end of the world they knew, how should they concern themselves for recording their success? There would be nobody for whom to record it. The amazing record contained in the Acts and the Letters of Paul is far more than we have in the circumstances any reason to expect. Yet about the time of Nero's persecution described by Tacitus, A.D. 64, there was what he calls a huge multitude of Christian believers in Rome that were actually cruelly put to death, not to mention those who escaped arrest, as most of them did.

The effect of Jesus' trial upon Peter was to drive him to deny his Master, not one but three times. One might suppose these were repetitions of one story by Peter on various occasions, but the words of Jesus on the way to the Mount of

Olives, Mark 14:26-31, preclude that. Peter's bold assurance broke down before the combined threat of the Jewish council and the Roman procurator, and he denied his connection with Jesus as vehemently as he had previously endorsed him.

Yet on the Sunday morning it is Peter to whom Jesus first appears, and who thus first arrives at the Resurrection faith, I Cor. 15:5: "He was seen by Cephas, and then by the Twelve." This is our most ancient record of those days, and comes straight from Paul, who got it from Peter himself, in those two weeks Paul spent with him, Gal. 1:18. Galatians itself was written in A.D. 52, long before any Gospel record had been written. So Peter's quick reactions again put him in the lead of his fellow apostles. If he was swift to deny he was also first to realize Jesus as still a living presence and declare it.

The closing verses of Mark in most Bibles, 16:9-20, are easily seen to have nothing to do with the Gospel of Mark or its narrative, and they are absent from the most ancient manuscripts. They do not give the sequel Mark's narrative anticipates and indeed demands—reunion in Galilee, Mark 14:28; 16:7. In fact, they clearly belong to some other book, and in at least one Armenian manuscript of Mark, the name of Ariston (meaning Aristion?) was found in the margin, as though the passage were taken from him. These verses certainly have no fitness at the end of Mark, and the hideous reference to believers taking up snakes in their hands, as a test of their faith (as it is so often understood), certainly strikes a false note in the teaching of Jesus. It was just the sort of thing Satan urged Jesus to do, in the second temptation, Matt. 4:7, and Jesus replied in the language of Deut. 6:16:

" 'You shall not try the Lord your God.' "

Matthew, who is following Mark closely here, Matt. 28:1, 5-8, goes on, vs. 16-20, to tell of just such a reunion in Galilee as Mark has twice forecast, and it is reasonable to suppose he got the account of the reunion in Galilee from the same book from which he got the double forecast of it, namely, Mark.

It would seem that Mark was soon on its way to being displaced by the new Gospel of Matthew, which was so largely based upon it, but which contained such a wealth of devotional and spiritual material not in Mark. This naturally caused Mark to go gradually out of use; everyone would prefer Matthew, with its richness in Jesus' teaching—the Sermon on the Mount, for example, with the Beatitudes, the Lord's Prayer and the Golden Rule, and much besides. So forty years later, when the great idea of uniting four Gospels in one publication brought about the Fourfold Gospel, it was not strange that all that could be found of Mark was one defective copy, from which the last column or two were missing.

Since Matthew has been following Mark so closely, phrase by phrase, Matt. 28:1-10, 16-20, it is not difficult to follow in the rest of chapter 28 the sequel of the story Mark has begun to tell—the story of reunion in Galilee. Put back into Marcan language, this would read:

"And Jesus himself met them, and said,

" 'Good morning!'

"And they went up to him and clasped his feet, and bowed to the ground before him. Jesus said to them,

" 'You need not be afraid. Go and tell my brothers to go to Galilee and they will see me there.'

"And they went with great joy, and ran to tell his disciples. And the eleven disciples went to Galilee to the mountain to which Jesus had directed them. There they saw him and bowed down before him. And Jesus came up to them and said,

" 'Go and preach the good news to all the heathen. I will always be with you, to the end.' "

If the reader has any doubt about this reconstruction of the long-lost ancient conclusion of Mark's Gospel, he can easily satisfy himself of its reasonableness by comparing Matthew, chapter 28, phrase by phrase with the Mark column in the *Harmony of the Synoptic Gospels*, by Professor Burton and myself (Scribner, 1917), or if he prefers, the same work in Greek (University of Chicago Press, 1920).

In point of religious experience, Peter was thus the leader of the Twelve more truly than he had ever been before; in the Acts of the Apostles, written about A.D. 90, probably at Ephesus, he is clearly so regarded. For the first twelve chapters, Peter occupies the center of the stage in the Acts, except for perhaps a little more than half of chapter 9, which tells the story of the conversion of Saul. In the momentous events and experiences that make up the extraordinary record of religious experience and development, Peter is clearly foremost. It is he who rallies the apostles and proposes that another be chosen to take the place of Judas. It is clear that the Twelve did not take this duty upon themselves, but it was shared by the whole Christian group at Jerusalem, numbering a hundred and twenty persons, men and women! The women who had followed Jesus' group from Galilee seem from the first to have met with the men and been reckoned as members of the group. We are struck with the presence of Jesus' mother Mary and of his brothers—already named in Mark 6:3 as James, Joses, Judas and Simon. James, the eldest, seems to have brought the family circle to Jerusalem at once and to have become a sort of honorary head of the Jerusalem church. When Peter began to be more active in what might be called wider missions, James passed into the position of practically heading the Jerusalem group.

It is Peter who rallies the brotherhood, Acts 1:15, to choose a successor to the traitor Judas. When the gift of the Holy Spirit fell upon the believers at Jerusalem some two months later, and the Jews of Jerusalem were so amazed by it, it was Peter who stood up and explained it as a fulfilment of the famous prophecy of Joel, 2:28-32, supported by various oracles from The Psalms. Peter ended by charging them with having refused and crucified their Messiah.

It was this address of Peter's that led to the first great enlargement of the diminutive Jerusalem group; Acts reports that three thousand people joined the Christian body that day. The believers now assumed the status of a new sect of Judaism, frequenting the Temple like other Jews, but living on a communistic basis, those who had property selling it for the general support. Jerusalem was not, and has seldom if ever been, a self-supporting city; it had no industries or natural resources. The Christian group must have proceeded on the expectation of the early return of Jesus and the End of the Age, if it looked ahead at all. The Jews received fairly regular support from Jews who had gone west into the Roman world and made money there. This was just what Paul sought to do for the Jerusalem church by his collections among the Christian groups in Corinth and Macedonia, II Corinthians, chapter 9.

The cure of a lame man at the Beautiful Gate of the Temple soon afterward drew a great crowd and led to a spirited address by Peter, calling upon the people to repent and accept Jesus as their Messiah, especially since God had raised him from the dead! This roused the high priests, and the apostles were promptly arrested, although many who had heard Peter at once accepted Jesus as their Messiah, increasing the Christian community by two thousand more.

At their examination next day by the authorities the apostles held their ground, and after a further warning they were released. The community of believers was further cheered by the generous action of Joseph of Cyprus, a Levite, who sold a piece of land and gave the money to the apostles to aid the community. Another man who pretended to do the same thing secretly withheld part of the price paid him, and was so sternly rebuked by Peter for it in open meeting that he fell down dead. His wife who joined him in this effort to deceive the apostles suffered the same fate, almost at the command of Peter. This was quite unlike any act or precept of Jesus; what it did recall was Elisha's cursing of the forty-two little boys who made fun of him and were immediately mangled by two she-bears out of the woods, II Kings, chapter 2. It is the absence of this sort of thing in the Gospels that is so striking. According to the Acts, Peter later on threatened Simon the magician with dire penalties at Samaria, 8:20.

These dreadful occurrences greatly increased the awe in which the apostles were held, and people began to be brought in from the country round about in the hope that Peter's shadow might fall on them and restore them to health. This aroused the Sadducees to rearrest Peter and some at least of the apostles, but they were mysteriously released in the night and reappeared at the Temple next morning, preaching as before. This led to their rearrest and rebuke, but Peter did not flinch, but repeated his belief that Jesus had been raised from the dead. The council threatened to kill the apostles, but Gamaliel, the well-known authority of the Pharisees, protested and warned the rulers that they might find themselves fighting God! So after flogging the apostles they warned them again and let them go.

What an extraordinary story, about a fisherman from Galilee, with a strong religious interest and tendency, it is true, but no rabbinic training! After a few months in the constant companionship of Jesus and the Twelve, followed by the

Resurrection experience, he became a man equal to facing the religious public of Jerusalem and the official heads of the Jewish religion on their own ground.

If, as the Acts says, the preaching about Jesus now went forward without interference in the Temple as well as in private houses, it can only mean that the Christian group is accepted as just another Jewish sect, not to be interfered with. The appointment of the seven deacons, however, to supervise the distribution of food among the groups of widows, especially those of Greek speech, brought Stephen into the picture. His assault upon the Jewish people for their rejection of the prophets, and Jesus too when he came, in- furiated the Jewish populace and they stoned him, under the supervision of Saul, who now appears upon the scene.

Stephen's speech and death usher in a dire persecution of the believers, in the course of which Peter was dispatched to Samaria to introduce the faith there. The persecution seems to have been of short duration, and when they were once more at peace, Peter traveled about among the Palestin- ian churches and found himself at Joppa. There he is sought out by messengers from a Roman captain named Cornelius, stationed at Caesarea, and a broadening and enlightening vision enables him to bring the gospel to this Roman officer and his household. Luke clearly intends this very detailed narrative, Acts, chapter 10, to convey the rapidly widening scope of the Christian public, in which even Peter, though specially designated apostle to the Jews, at once took an active and successful part. That the language barrier meant nothing to Peter, in talking Greek to this Roman officer, is natural in the Acts, which understood ecstatic speaking (I Corinthians, chapter 12) to be talking in foreign languages, Acts 2:6. The meaning of the incident is clearly that Peter was already coming to realize the world-wide program and future of the Christian gospel.

Peter's vision of the cleanness even of heathen food reflects his enlarging view and prepares him for the great Roman mission in which his work was later to culminate. The attack of Herod Agrippa I upon the Jerusalem church, which resulted in the execution of the Apostle James the son of Zebedee, also threatened Peter. In fact, he was arrested, but was strangely enabled to escape and report his safety to the anxious brotherhood. Only the death of Herod stopped the persecution, A.D. 44. Peter is mentioned fifty-five times in the first twelve chapters of the Acts, and once later, in chapter 15. It is Paul who now takes the stage, being mentioned one hundred and twenty-four times in the sixteen chapters, 13-28.

Paul, in A.D. 52, in writing to the Galatians, speaks of Peter as divinely actuated to be an apostle to the Jews and as regarded in Jerusalem as one of the pillars of the church. In fact, James, the Lord's brother, and Peter and John "who were regarded as pillars of the church," Gal. 2:9, pledged their full co-operation to Barnabas and Paul in their missionary work among the heathen, with the understanding that the three, James, Peter and John, were to carry on the mission to the Jews.

Paul goes on with a dramatic story, 2:11-14, of how a little later Peter visited Antioch and bravely ate with the heathen, that is, in disregard of the traditional Jewish food regulations. After the arrival there of some emissaries of James, Peter began to draw back and hold aloof from the heathen converts, "for fear of the party of circumcision." Paul goes on to say that the other Jewish Christians, carried away by Peter's recognized position in the Christian movement, "followed his example in concealing their real views, so that even Barnabas was carried away by their pose." Paul met the situation with great boldness, for he realized its vital importance to the Christian mission. When he saw, as he puts it, "that they were not straightforward about the truth of the

good news, I said to Cephas, right before them all, 'If you
live like a heathen'"—that is, in the matter of clean and
unclean food—"'and not like a Jew, though you are a Jew
yourself, why should you try to make the heathen live like
Jews?'"

That is, Peter had been eating with the converted heathen
and eating what they ate, without scruple, but when the
agents of James came on the scene at Antioch he weakened
and began to stop eating with the converted heathen. Yet
James was not an apostle—one of the Twelve—nor had he,
as far as we can learn or judge, followed Jesus and sustained
him in his course until after his earthly ministry was over and
the church had begun to rise in Jerusalem, when James had
left Nazareth and joined it. His influence in it seems to have
been reactionary, that is, in the direction of letting the church
become simply another sect of Judaism. Yet Paul on his
return from Damascus, soon after his conversion, when he
had his historic visit with Peter, Gal. 1:18, 19, had met James,
the Lord's brother, so that he and Peter were Paul's oldest
Christian friends.

Whether or not Paul's admonition won Peter to his
position at Antioch, it certainly prevailed with him later, for
Peter seems to have succeeded Paul in his mission to the
heathen. While we cannot date the so-called Acts of Peter
earlier than A.D. 200, five Christian writings of the end of the
first and beginning or middle of the second century provide
us with important allusions to his work and fate.

1. The *First Letter of Clement*, written in Rome, about
A.D. 95, says, in chapter 5:

> But to pass from ancient examples (he has just been speaking
> of Abel, Jacob, Moses, and David), let us come to those who
> have most recently proved champions; let us take up the noble
> examples of our own generation. Because of jealousy and envy

the greatest and most upright pillars of the church were persecuted, and competed unto death. Let us bring before our eyes
the good apostles—Peter, who, because of unrighteous jealousy
endured not one or two but numerous trials, and so bore a martyr's witness and went to the glorious place that he deserved.

He goes on to speak of Paul in similar terms.

2. There can be little doubt that the Revelation, 11:3,
written before A.D. 96, has the same great martyrs in view:
John is told:

" 'I will permit my two witnesses, clothed in sackcloth, to
prophesy for 1,260 days.' " (The Greek word for "witnesses"
is "martyrs.")

The prophet continues, v. 7:

"When they finish their testimony, the animal that comes
up out of the abyss will make war on them and conquer
them and kill them, and their bodies will lie in the street of
the great city that is figuratively called Sodom and Egypt—
where their Lord also was crucified. For three days and a
half, men of all peoples, tribes, languages, and nations will
look at their bodies, and will not let them be buried. . . . For
these two prophets were a torment to the inhabitants of the
earth. After three days and a half, . . . they heard a loud voice
from heaven say to them,

" 'Come up here.'

"And they went up to heaven in a cloud, before the eyes
of their enemies."

Difficult as this passage is, it must refer to the martyrdoms
of Peter and Paul in Rome. The prophet looks forward to the
punishment of the city and its population in an earthquake.
Perhaps he had in mind the eruption of Vesuvius in A.D. 79,
and the heavy loss of life in what he might well regard as one
of Rome's suburbs, though Pompeii and Herculaneum were
as far away as Naples.

3. The First Letter of Peter, written about A.D. 95 to
counteract the danger created by the Revelation, of making
Christianity a rebellious movement, speaking for the Roman
church claims the authority of Peter, 1:1, and calls upon its
readers to "submit . . . to the emperor, as supreme, and to
governors, as sent by him to punish evil-doers, and to encourage those who do right. . . . Love the brotherhood, be
reverent to God, respect the emperor," 2:13-17.

"Your sister-church in Babylon, chosen like you, and Mark
my son wish to be remembered to you." The allusion to
Rome, and to Peter's connection with Mark through Mark's
publication of the Gospel based on Peter's memories is unmistakable. Mark is a Roman Gospel, I Peter 5:13. Peter is
represented as writing in the name of the Roman church.
Babylon, we need not remind the reader, had long meant
Rome. Think of this equivalence in Baruch, about A.D. 70,
the Revelation, the Letter of Jeremiah and Second Esdras.
This posthumous reference to Peter-Mark-Rome was clearly
meant to designate Peter as the source, Mark as the writer,
and Rome as the place of writing of the Gospel of Mark.

4. The Gospel of John (written about A.D. 110), 21:19, as
the Evangelist is careful to point out, refers to Peter's
martyrdom. "He said this to show the kind of death [cruci-
fixion?] by which Peter was to honor God."

5. The Second Letter of Peter, written about A.D. 150, in
1:13-15, says: "Yet I think it right, as long as I live in my
present tent, to arouse you by a reminder, for I know that I
must soon put it away, as our Lord Jesus Christ has shown
me." This is clearly a reference to John 21:18 and alludes to
the apostle's part, so essential, although involuntary, to the
composition of the Gospel of Mark. We have no reason to
suppose Peter had any idea of anyone's recording what he
said in his preaching, but the fact that this is the kind of

thing he preached throws a great light upon his ministry, no matter how selective Mark may have felt it necessary to be, in the later writing of his Gospel. We do not imagine Mark wrote down from the wealth of his memories everything he could remember that Peter said; he was clearly limiting himself to what Peter had quite incidentally told of his memories of the acts, words and experiences of Jesus. In doing this he made a contribution to all subsequent Christianity that was of incalculable value. Yet the writer of the letter went so far as to say: "I will also take care that after I am gone you will be able at any time to call these things to mind. For they were no fictitious stories that we followed"—going on with an allusion to the Transfiguration experience, of Mark 9:2-7. Here II Peter makes the voice from heaven say:

" 'This is my Son, my Beloved! He is my Chosen!' "
while the Gospel of Mark gives the oracle as,

" 'This is my Son, my Beloved! Listen to him!' "

The date of Peter's death, in all probability by martyrdom, is much debated. It hinges upon the time of his departure from Jerusalem and his going to Rome. Peter's mission, as Paul saw it, was to the Jews, Gal. 2:7-10, and in the Gospel of Mark, which so clearly shows its Petrine source and character, we read, 13:14-16, " 'As soon as you see the dreadful desecration standing where he has no right to stand' (the reader must take note of this), 'then those who are in Judea must fly to the hills.' " It is impossible to suppose that Peter himself remained in Jerusalem after the Roman invasion of A.D. 66; the Christians must have been expressly warned in his teaching, as later in his Gospel, 13:14, 15, to make their escape from the city before it was surrounded. The only question is, how long before? Did Peter leave Jerusalem and seek his Jewish missionary public in Rome before, or after, the Neronian persecution of 64? There was, of course, a

substantial Jewish community in the capital and when Jerusalem became impossible, where else would Peter have
turned for his new headquarters, as the apostle to the Jews,
as Paul frankly considered him, Gal. 2:7? That Peter was
taken there as a prisoner is unlikely; he was no Roman citizen
as Paul was, who could appeal to the emperor's court! The
tradition is that Peter died by crucifixion, like any ordinary
malefactor.

Yet it is not likely that he was already in Rome when Paul
was taken there about A.D. 59, since neither Luke in the Acts
nor Paul in his letters written from Rome—Colossians, Philemon, Philippians—alludes to Peter's presence there. Since
Peter was recognized among Christians as the apostle to the
Jews, Paul could hardly be represented as contacting the
Jewish leaders in Rome (Acts 28:17-28) without some allusion to Peter's presence in Rome if he was already there.
Peter must have gone there after Paul's death and before the
outbreak of the Jewish war, or at the very beginning of it.
If, as some suppose, he perished in the persecution by Nero,
so strikingly described by Tacitus and also, as I believe
in Heb. 10:32-34, that would fix his death in that year. Recent
excavations in the Vatican hill encourage the belief that it
was there Peter was crucified, but his burial place was doubtless elsewhere. It was as the scene of his *martyrdom* that the
spot was hallowed.

These excavations of the Vatican hill lead to the conclusion
that it was a place of execution and owed its later sanctity to
the fact that it was there that Peter suffered martyrdom; his
burial place being at the time a matter of indifference. As
the place of Peter's martyrdom, as his figure loomed larger
with the spread of Christianity at Rome, it soon came to
possess a high degree of sanctity, so that the early bishops
of Rome, later known as popes, were buried there, and a

church dedicated to St. Peter was erected. That Peter himself was buried there is highly improbable. Moreover, the
primitive Christian expectation of the end of the world at an
early date and the resurrection of the dead definitely
diminished concern for the location of their places of burial.
There had been little interest in the location of Paul's grave,
about A.D. 60, and there seems to have been little immediate
interest in that of Peter.

6

PETER AND HIS PARTNERS

~~~~~~~~

Peter in the Gospels

THE WAY in which Jesus calls Peter, or Simon, to him in Mark 1:16-18 must mean that they already know each other and are friends, for Simon and Andrew immediately obey his summons. This must mean that they have met at John's camp meetings over by the Jordan, and it is Mark's idea that Jesus began his work after John's arrest, 1:14. Up to that time he was content to leave the task of religious reformation to John and his message of repentance, but when John was silenced by being imprisoned, Jesus takes the stage to set up the Kingdom of God on earth. From their talks with him before, Simon and Andrew are prepared to join Jesus' movement as soon as he summons them, and this they unhesitatingly do.

Simon was a fisherman of Capernaum, on the Sea of Galilee. His father's name was John, John 1:42; 21:15-17. He and his brother Andrew occupied a house in Capernaum; Peter was married, and his wife's mother lived with them; Jesus cured her of a fever when he first came to live with them, for he seems to have made their house his home all through his Galilean preaching period.

60

Luke tells us that James and John, the two sons of Zebedee, whom Jesus called at the same time to be his followers, and later to be his apostles, were their partners. Mark says James and John had hired men working for them in their fishing, 1:20, when they dropped everything to follow the call of Jesus.

Dr. Henry Van Dyke once told me that when he first caught sight of the Sea of Galilee he stopped on the shore, got out his fishing rod and tackle, and waded right into the lake to try his luck in those thrice historic waters! The fisherman in him could not resist them. He had artificial bait, but it was enough and he caught a surprising number of fish, most if not all of them totally unknown to his fishing experience, extraordinarily wide as it was. The Galilee fishing business in which so many of the disciples were engaged was more than a sport or a small business; it was an industry, as the town of Tarichaea on its southern shore proves; *tarichos* means "smoked fish," and it was evidently a place named from the doubtless considerable industry established there. The business of drying, curing and smoking the fish from the lake, not merely for local consumption but for the country round, had given the town its name, and it was only two or three hours' sail from Capernaum and Bethsaida.

The Gospel of John speaks of Jesus' giving the name Peter, or in the Aramaic they all talked, Kepha (Greek, *Kephas;* Latin, *Cephas*) to Simon when he met him at John's camp meetings, 1:42. But the Gospel of Matthew, 16:16-18, connects it with Peter's startling recognition of Jesus as the Christ. From the time Jesus calls them ashore at Capernaum, Peter is wholly identified with Jesus' movement and acts as his host and chief assistant. He is his boatman, and Jesus practically lives in his boat.

Not only in these practical ways but in their conversations and discussions, Peter appears as the spokesman of the apostles and their acknowledged leader. We get the impression that he was about Jesus' age, not far from thirty, that he was quick in speech, and impulsive, as when he said at Caesarea Philippi, and he was the first man to say it,

" 'You are the Christ!' "

A week later he proposed that they build huts for Jesus, Moses and Elijah and stay on the Mount of Transfiguration, Mark 9:2-5.

A few weeks later, after the Last Supper, Peter declares, " 'Even if they all desert you, I will not!' "

And Jesus vigorously rejoins,

" 'This very night . . . you yourself will disown me three times!' "

But Peter insisted upon his unshakable devotion:

" 'If I have to die with you, I will never disown you!' "

But they all said the same thing. Yet the next morning, Peter's own memoirs record Jesus' terrible words came true, in Peter's denial. But it must be observed, Peter was the only one of the Twelve near enough to him even to deny him! These final chapters of Mark, 14-16, are heroic tragedy at its greatest, by virtue of their sheer truth to the terrible story they have to tell. Such were Peter's recollections of that tremendous climax as he uttered them a generation later to the Christian believers at Rome. We cannot miss the autobiography of Peter, between the lines, unsparingly told.

Yet the last words of the young man at the tomb, Mark 16:7, direct the mourning women to the disciples and Peter, as now their head, to bid them to seek Jesus in Galilee, as he had previously told them to do.

Some of this story we may suppose Peter told to Paul, in the two weeks he spent with Cephas, as recorded in Gal. 1:18. I can see no more probable explanation of the whole tremendous narrative in Mark, than what Mark could remem-

ber after Peter's martyrdom, of Peter's own oft-repeated
story of those momentous days. It was the peculiar distinction of Peter that he was the first to hail Jesus as the Christ,
the Messiah of Jewish hope and expectation, Mark 8:29. This
salutation is hailed with enthusiastic approval in Matthew,
16:17, but in Mark's account, which we must consider nearest
to the actual occurrence, Jesus merely warns them not to
say this about him to anyone. It is no mere coincidence that
the first man to recognize Jesus as the Messiah of Jewish
expectation is also the first man to realize him as a living
presence, at the Resurrection. In both these great experiences Peter led the way for the Early Church.

Peter and Paul

When Paul after his conversion and work in Damascus
returned to Jerusalem, probably in A.D. 36, he was disowned
by the Jews, and yet not acceptable to the Christian believers
who could not forget his leading part in the stoning of
Stephen, the first Christian martyr. It was Barnabas who
reached him and introduced him to the apostles and became
his lifelong friend, Acts 9:27. Paul speaks in Gal. 1:18 particularly of meeting Cephas, whom he speaks of also as Peter.
This was a meeting of the utmost importance to Paul, as
Peter was possessed of a wealth of personal information of
Jesus' words and sayings, some of which he could not help
sharing with this new convert who had everything to learn
about the historical Jesus; there were as yet no books about
him, such as we possess in the Gospels. It was probably then
that Paul learned more definitely of such moving scenes as
the Last Supper and exactly what Jesus said in those tragic
moments, I Cor. 11:24, 25; Mark 14:22-24. The words are
not identical, but the identification of the bread with his

body and the wine with his blood is unmistakable. These are our first accounts of the Last Supper and what Jesus meant it to be.

Peter and Paul met again more than once, and not always in agreement, Gal. 2:9, 11, 14. Paul speaks in I Cor. 9:5 of Peter as taking a Christian wife about with him, apparently in his missionary travels; her mother, we remember, was cured of a fever by Jesus, Mark 1:31, the first miracle! In the later story of Peter's martyrdom this heroic woman is again mentioned, for as she was being led to martyrdom Peter called to her comfortingly, "O thou, remember the Lord!" This is told by both Clement of Alexandria and Eusebius.

Professor Cullmann, the Swiss scholar, in his recent work on Peter, infers from the fact that Peter is not mentioned in Romans, chapter 16, that Peter was not in Rome when Paul wrote the letter in A.D. 56. But this loses sight of the fact that some identifiable people mentioned in the chapter are quite manifestly in Ephesus, not in Rome at all—Prisca, Aquila, Epaenetus, so that the Letter of Introduction for Phoebe is evidently meant for the church there, not at Rome. When the Pauline letters were collected and published at Ephesus, soon after A.D. 90, this short letter, too brief to stand alone, was appended to Romans to preserve it. It was obviously a letter to a church well-known to Paul, for he knows its household groups, and he singles them out one after another, for he is introducing Phoebe of Cenchreae to them, with the evident wish that they will look after her and see to her security and comfort while she is among them. Paul had no such knowledge of the church at Rome, years before he went there. A woman traveling alone about the Roman world needed such help, when hotels or what passed for them were often of very questionable character. This was where Christian hospitality came into the picture so importantly, and Romans, chapter 16, notably illustrates it. More

than this, the great doxology, vs. 25-27, in later manuscripts
at the end of chapter 16, is now seen in the Michigan manuscript to be at the end of chapter 15, and thus to precede the
Letter of Introduction for Phoebe and conclude the epistle.
This manuscript is far the oldest one of Paul that we possess,
the best German authorities assigning it to about the year
200! So internal evidence (the sense of the passage) and
external evidence (the testimony of the oldest manuscript)
here combine to show that Rom. 16:1-23 is a separate letter
of introduction for Phoebe to the church at Ephesus.

It is not unlikely that Peter went to Rome under the two-
fold impact of the fearful blow Nero's persecution of A.D. 64
had dealt the church there, plus the evidently certain pros-
pect of the approaching Jewish revolt against Rome, which
broke out in 66. This would place his arrival there with much
probability soon after 64.

Recent excavations beneath St. Peter's and about it seem
to prove that the Vatican hill was the scene of Peter's execution and martyrdom rather than his burial place. It came to
be a favorite burial place for Christians of distinction on that
account, the place where he suffered being rightly considered
of more interest and significance than the place of his burial,
even if the latter were known. Ordinarily the burial of
victims of the Roman authority would be done by the
servants of the state, with little opportunity for private
interference; it was only by an influential appeal to the
governor that Jesus' body was rescued for private interment,
in the Gospels. We have no record of any such efforts in
the case of Peter, and indeed who was there to interfere with
an application for special treatment? Nor were the primitive
believers with their keen expectation of the quick end of the
world likely to be concerned with such matters as grave-
locations of Paul or Peter. Clearly it is the place of Peter's
death, especially in so extraordinary a martyrdom, that

would have interested the ancient church, even as it interests us today. Subsequent piety made of the spot a favorite place of burial, as the recent excavations have shown, certainly by the early years of the second century; and there many of the early bishops of Rome, later known as popes, found their resting places.

Peter was the most dynamic of the twelve apostles, the readiest and the most outspoken. He was the first to recognize Jesus as the Messiah of Jewish expectation, which profession Jesus said would be the basis of his church. Not *petros*, a rock, but *petra*, rock.

Yet also most impulsive, too ready to turn around and rebuke his Master, and even in the supreme crisis deny him! It is just this too, too human blend of traits that makes Peter the most appealing figure of all the apostles; this is the terrific realism of the Gospels. So Mark becomes in a secondary sense a record of Peter, the eyewitness and relater of it all! This is not only the story, it also has significance as Peter's reaction to it. This is how Peter understood it and afterward reported it in his preaching.

Only a fraction of what Peter said in his Roman discourses was remembered by Mark and embodied in his Gospel and its manifest consciousness of the Jewish war with Rome, Mark 13:7, 8, 14-19, strongly points to a date around 70 for that Gospel; the war of 66-70 if not already over is near its end. It made a terrible impression upon the Jewish public all over the Roman world. Josephus, a veteran of it, wrote his account of it in Rome, while on a Roman literary pension designed to foster Greek literary writing, twenty-five years later.

Peter and Mark

The Gospel of Mark, the earliest of the Gospels, has its action after the first page so completely in the presence of

Simon the fisherman of Capernaum that we cannot escape
the conviction that he was directly or indirectly its source
and narrator. Jesus evidently knew these two brothers Simon
and Andrew and called to them as an old friend, or at least
as a familiar acquaintance might do. It seems clear that he
had known them before, probably at John's meetings on the
Jordan, before Antipas had put John in prison. Indeed, it
was this interruption of John's work that Jesus had taken as
the signal for him to begin his preaching, Mark 1:14. The
Gospel of John definitely says that Jesus met Simon and
Andrew at Bethany beyond Jordan, among John's followers.
In fact, Jesus is said to have given Simon the name Peter
when he first met him. Clearly the two brothers were already
friends and adherents of Jesus well before he saw them fishing on the Sea of Galilee and made them actively his
followers.

Christian tradition connects the writing of Mark with
Rome, where Peter's last preaching and his martyrdom most
probably occurred, and where Peter's memory has been most
assiduously cherished from the second century until today.
This fact has combined with his vital part in the Gospel
narrative to enhance his pre-eminence among the Twelve.
Jesus' glad response to his bold expression of faith in him,
hailing him as the man of rock among the disciples, strongly
encouraged this attitude, even though at another time Jesus
rebuked him just as sternly:

" 'Get out of my sight, you Satan! for you do not side with
God, but with men.' " Words all the more terrible, since not
long before Peter had been the first to hail him as the Christ,
Mark 8:29, 33.

Certainly Rome seems to have become the repository of
memories of Peter, and to have become the champion of his
greatness. This in itself is a strong reinforcement of the
tradition of his ministry there, ending in his martyrdom. That

Peter would have left Jerusalem about A.D. 66 at the latest is strongly suggested by Jesus' words in Mark 13:14, warning his followers to leave the city in haste when the Temple is desecrated and the heathen take possession of the city. But where were they to go? No serious tradition connects Peter's later days with any place but Rome, and he may well have gone there. Its importance in the missionary campaign was obvious; there had been a church there for at least ten years; Paul had written a letter to the Christians in Rome A.D. 56 and had suffered martyrdom there in 60 or soon after. In 64 occurred Nero's outbreak against the Christians of Rome, on the pretext that they had burned the city or part of it. The story is briefly but powerfully told in Tacitus, *Annals* xv, 44.

7

THE APOSTLES AND THE GOSPELS

The Oral Gospel of the Apostles

WE HAVE SEEN how the earliest Gospel arose in Jewish fashion, as an oral formulation of what was remembered by one of his apostles, said to have been Matthew; such at least is the statement of Papias, of Hierapolis, in Phrygia, about A.D. 130-140. Matthew, he says, composed the Sayings (Logia) in the Aramaic language, and each one translated them (into Greek?) as best he could. We have seen how Luke in the opening sentence of his Gospel seems to refer to this sort of thing when he says, "Just as the original eye-witnesses who became teachers of the message have handed it down to us," Luke 1:2. The way in which some early fragments of teaching and tradition are given in Paul seems to corroborate this impression.

Thus in I Cor. 11:23-25, written probably in A.D. 53, Paul tells the Corinthians about the origin of the Lord's Supper; long before there was as far as we know any written Gospel: "For I myself received from the Lord the account that I passed on to you, that the Lord Jesus the night he was betrayed took some bread and gave thanks for it and then broke it in pieces, saying,

" 'This is my body which takes your place. Do this in memory of me.' He took the cup, too, after supper, in the same way, saying,

" 'This cup is the new agreement ratified by my blood. Whenever you drink it, do so in memory of me.' " It would seem that this was part of the teaching Peter had given Paul when they spent some days together during Paul's short stay in Jerusalem on his return from Damascus, Gal. 1:18.

Later in the same letter, I Cor. 15:3-7, Paul gives the account of the death and Resurrection of Jesus that he had received, evidently from Peter, in the two weeks he had spent with him in Jerusalem, probably in A.D. 36. This was plainly an unwritten communication, handed on by word of mouth in the habitual Jewish manner of the times.

The Acts speaks of "remembering the words of the Lord Jesus," 20:35, quoting words that have not been found in any written Gospel, " 'It makes one happier to give than to be given to.' " Clement of Rome, about A.D. 95, twice quotes sayings of Jesus not exactly like any in our Gospels, introducing both quotations with the words, "Remember the words of the Lord Jesus." Polycarp of Smyrna, writing to the Philippians about A.D. 107-117, speaks in just the same way in introducing sayings ascribed to Jesus: "Remember what the Lord said." The use by two different writers of the word "remember" in introducing these sayings further encourages the conclusion that they are both quoting an oral, not a written, gospel. We may suppose it was an Aramaic compend of what Jesus' first and nearest followers thought his most characteristic acts and sayings, and that in Galilee and Judea it served a high practical religious purpose. Its part in the religious experience and training of Paul is very clear; it was the only "gospel" he ever had, and those two weeks at the feet of Peter were of untold value in Paul's religious development. But a generation later, when Christianity was sweeping through the Greek world, the times demanded a written record, and that led to a whole series of them, in which we still rejoice.

What did this written record contain? We can only say it included these half-dozen facts and utterances reported by Paul in writing to Corinth, and then to the Galatians, and in his farewell to the Ephesian elders who came over to Miletus to say good-by. We find these words few, but immensely precious, uttered or written by Paul in A.D. 52, 53 and 56.

Hardly less interesting are the echoes of the Sayings found in Clement and Polycarp. Clement, writing from Rome in his letter to the Corinthians, tells them, 13:1, 2:

> Especially remember the words of the Lord Jesus that he uttered when he was teaching gentleness and patience. For this is what he said: "Show mercy, that you may be shown mercy. Forgive, that you may be forgiven. As you do, so it will be done to you; as you give, so it will be given to you; as you judge, so you will be judged; as you are kind, so kindness will be shown to you. The measure you use will be used in measuring to you.

We recognize at once in this the teaching we find in Matt. 5:7; 6:14, 15; 7:1, 2, 12; Luke 6:31, 36-38.

Again in I Clement 46:7, 8, we read:

> Remember the words of our Lord Jesus, for he said, "Alas for that man! It would have been better for him if he had never been born than to make one of my chosen fall! He might better have had a millstone hung around his neck and have been sunk in the sea, than to pervert one of my chosen."

This recalls Mark 14:21; Matt. 26:24; Luke 22:22; 17:2, as well as Matt. 18:6; Mark 9:42.

Similarly Polycarp of Smyrna, in writing to the Philippians, has this remarkable passage, 2:3:

Remembering what the Lord said when he taught: "Do not judge, so that you may not be judged, forgive, and you will be forgiven; have mercy, so that you may be shown mercy; with the measure you use, men will measure back to you; and blessed are the poor and those who are persecuted for their uprightness, for the kingdom of God belongs to them."

This again is very much like Mark 7:1, 2; Luke 6:36-38, and in its second part, Luke 6:20; Matt. 5:3, 10. In all these passages it will be noted the leaders are called upon to "Remember the words of the Lord Jesus"; to remember what the Lord said, in a way quite different from the usual way of referring to a written gospel or letter.

Simon Peter and the Gospel According to Mark

It is a wonderful thought that we may reasonably regard the Gospel of Mark as really that of Jesus' closest disciple, Simon Peter, afterward almost dictated to and translated by John Mark, the attendant of Paul and the interpreter of Peter. In fact, we may do so after the few opening verses, 1-8, telling of John the Baptist's appearance, as Isaiah had foretold, with his preaching of repentance and baptism in order to obtain the forgiveness of sins, and his camp meetings, as we would call them, on the lower Jordan, his Elijah-like clothing and food, and his prediction of a Mightier One to come, who would baptize them in the very Spirit of God.

Simon must have been among John's hearers and followers on the Jordan; he certainly is the first to report the baptism of Jesus and how the Spirit of God came down and took possession of him then and there. The other Evangelists say the Spirit came "upon" him, but Mark says it came "into" him. Luke must have understood it so, for he says, 4:1, that Jesus returned from the Jordan "full of the holy Spirit."

Not that Simon Peter ever thought of writing a book; the time was short—much too short for the writing and publishing of books, even about something as momentous as the life and deeds of Jesus. No, Simon Peter preached, finally at Rome, where the Christian group remained a Greek-speaking and writing community until the middle of the third century. Peter was not at home in Greek; his native Aramaic was his language, and in that he preached to Jews and Greeks at Rome. For the benefit of the Greeks, who came to form the majority of the Christian group there, young men who knew both languages well would stand beside Peter as he sat preaching and, like interpreters today, translate what he said sentence by sentence into Greek for those who did not know Aramaic. Peter's narrative was constantly interrupted, we must suppose, with appeal, reproof, argument and entreaty, for it was not narrative but preaching; the narratives were probably only occasional interruptions, though of the most telling kind. But all this, reminiscence and entreaty alike, Peter surely used in preaching the gospel to the interested Greeks of Rome. Ten or more years before, Paul had written them a wonderful letter, which they still prized and kept in their church chest, perhaps reading it in church occasionally. Twenty-five years later it was hunted out and published in the first collection of Paul's letters, to which we still owe so much.

There were no written gospels anywhere when Peter was preaching the gospel to the Romans in the early or middle sixties. And with what rapt attention they must have listened to this closest companion of Jesus, in his walks about Galilee and his voyages on the lake, always in Peter's boat; why, he even lived in Peter's house! Peter knew him as no one else could possibly have known him, in those most significant months of his life. To have heard Peter tell of him must have been something every Roman auditor remembered all the rest of his life.

But suddenly the preaching stops. Peter is arrested, martyred, crucified. There was no long elaborate trial, such as Paul had. Peter was no Roman citizen. The agents of Nero pick him up and hurry him off to execution, and he is gone! And with him the most important memories of Jesus in the world perish and disappear. The first reaction of the Christians was horror, grief and pity. But the lasting one was a great regret that all his precious memories of Jesus' life and action and teaching were gone, irrecoverably gone, from the world. They would never again hear those wonderful narratives, so simple and yet so moving, which they had so enjoyed hearing from Peter's lips.

Into this situation steps Mark. He was a young man from Jerusalem, an assistant, though not always a satisfactory one, of Paul, Acts 13:13; 15:37, 38, but he afterward redeemed himself and stood by Paul to the last in Rome, Col. 4:10; Philemon 24. He had been one of the young men who had been interpreting for Peter in his preaching to the Greek believers at Rome, and he had so often cast Peter's recollections of Jesus in Greek terms for the congregation that many of them were still quite definite in his memory. When he began to read these remembered stories to the Roman congregation, perhaps their collective memories helped him to perfect his narrative. The units of it were naturally brief and in a way complete in themselves. But when the climax was reached in the terrible story of chapters 14, 15 and 16, the simple narrative rises into high tragedy, unequaled in the literature of the world. The elaborate sixteenth-century language of our traditional Bibles has muffled and obscured the staggering power of these chapters, as they had come from the lips of Peter and now echoed from the hand of Mark. So the story that begins so simply rises toward the end to great heights, not through any device of literary crafts-manship but just by virtue of the story it has to tell.

The story never names itself as Peter's, but who else but Jesus was always present, and often as leading questioner? Peter is clearly the leading if not the sole authority for the story. Yet he is not the actual narrator. He is always spoken of in the third person. What clinches the evidence for him as the source of most if not all of the stirring story is the frank, unflinching account of Peter's denial! In the moment of crisis he had failed his Master. Who but Peter could have told this? For anyone else to tell it would have been incredible. Only Peter could tell that fearful story, and from his lips it would be indescribably moving. Who, after hearing that confession, could fail to get up and confess his sins? But for anyone else to put in circulation such a story, even if true, would be an utterly unchristian thing to do.

About A.D. 1200 the books of the Bible, in the Latin version then current in Europe, were divided, probably by Stephen Langton, afterward Archbishop of Canterbury but then stationed in Paris, into the chapters so convenient and familiar. It was not always soundly done, as when he broke off the seventh day, the climax of the Creation week, and put it into the second chapter of Genesis, although if there is a literary unit anywhere in the whole world of literature it is the seven days of the Creation week! Langton broke Mark into sixteen chapters, but the loosely connected incidents and episodes, long and short, of which it consists can easily be reckoned at nearer three times that number. These are loosely connected, and yet they reveal a striking and convincing continuity. Modern learning has even detected a tragic strain running through the book which, though sometimes denied, can hardly be missed.

It is the imprisonment of John the Baptist and the interruption of his preaching that stirs Jesus to begin to preach.

His message is that the time has come and the reign of God is to begin; men must repent and accept this good news. He proposes to set up the Kingdom of God on earth! He soon offends the Pharisees and they, with the adherents of Herod Antipas, the governor of Galilee, begin to plan to kill Jesus.

This leads Jesus to withdraw to the less populous eastern shore of the lake, Mark 3:7, and to select twelve of his followers to be his closer companions and messengers. There is a hint here of what Isaiah had done centuries before. While Isaiah's mission had ended in eclipse and martyrdom, his magnificent work had survived, for his pupils had preserved and circulated his recorded message in what became one of the greatest books of the Bible; indeed, one of the greatest ever written. Without Isaiah's disciples his work could hardly have survived. Was Jesus already facing the very real possibility that his own work would be cut short?

A little later, 7:24, Jesus again gives ground before his enemies in Galilee and withdraws from the dominions of Antipas to the region of Tyre and Sidon. He wishes no one to know of his presence there and makes a roundabout return to the shore of the lake. In 8:27 he retreats a third time to the region of Caesarea Philippi, north of Galilee. It was then that Peter declared him to be the Messiah, 8:29. The Transfiguration experience follows, 9:2-8.

Then, in 10:1, Jesus boldly assumes the offensive; he sets forth for Judea and Jerusalem, there to offer himself and his message to the Jewish people at their great Passover festival. He eats the Passover supper with his disciples, chapter 14, making this Last Supper his own memorial, vs. 22-25.

The betrayal, trial, Crucifixion and Resurrection follow in a fast-moving narrative of heroic tragedy unequaled in the world. What shall we say of the fisherman apostle whose sermons, remembered after his death, provided such materials? No wonder Peter towers above his fellow Galileans in his influence through the long centuries. Think of what the mere memories of his preaching have meant to the world and religion! It is an overwhelming thought.

Mark's little book of forty pages became the pattern Gospel and was actually wrought into the fabric of the other Gospels of the first century. Fifteen-sixteenths reappear in Matthew, and two-thirds are embodied in Luke. Of course, both these Evangelists added much besides, for their Gospels are half again as long as Mark. So the indirect influence of Mark has been even greater than his direct effect, through the use the great Evangelists who followed him have made of the materials his book supplied.

It is very difficult to extricate Peter's biography from these chapters of Mark, for it is so essentially the story of Jesus. It is for that and not as material for his own biography that Peter told the stories over and over again to his Greek audiences in Rome, until his interpreter formed so definite a pattern of them in his memory that he could write such a record as the Gospel of Mark before his recollections faded. The sudden and dramatic martyrdom of Peter awoke the Christian believers of Rome to the fact that their knowledge of the life and teaching of Jesus rested largely on what he had told them. So with Peter's disappearance from the scene they came to realize the great loss they had sustained; they would never again hear the wonderful accounts of his walks and talks with Jesus, in his brief ministry in Galilee and Judea.

It was then that Mark's idea of assembling what he could of these stories from his own memories of hearing and translating them as Peter's interpreter came to his mind, and led to the writing of the Gospel of Mark. This not only served the immediate needs of the Roman Christians but was of the utmost value to later gospel writers. In fact, it created the gospel type of literature and served as model and source for Matthew and then for Luke, giving each of those Evangelists not only his main literary gospel pattern but much of his most primitive and authentic material as well, since as we have seen, fifteen-sixteenths (or as Streeter says, nineteen-twentieths) of Mark reappears in Matthew and three-fifths of Mark meets us again in Luke. Luke's indebtedness is the more striking, as, unlike Matthew, practically everything he takes over from Mark he uses in Mark's own order.

Peter's great literary achievement, then, was an unconscious and even a posthumous one, for in his Aramaic preaching to the Roman believers he was quite unconsciously laying the foundation for the whole gospel movement with its tremendous consequences for religious life and history. The two letters written in Peter's name long afterward contain references to Mark and Rome, I Peter 5:13; II Peter 1:15-18.

Dr. Horton once wrote a book on *The Cartoons of St. Mark,* viewing that Gospel's contents as chiefly a series of great scenes or pictures, swiftly drawn, each setting forth some pregnant act of Jesus, with all its larger implications. From this approach consider their themes: the baptism; the casting out of the foul spirit, in the synagogue; the cure of Peter's mother-in-law; the sick cured at Peter's door; the cleansing of the leper (So much for the first chapter!); the paralytic lowered through the roof; the call of Levi the tax collector; the dinner with the tax collectors; why the disciples were not keeping the fast; the Sabbath walk through the wheat fields; the cure of the withered hand; the retreat from the Herodians; the choosing of the Twelve; the charge of serving Beelzebub; his real brothers and sisters; the preaching from the boat; the Parable of the Sower; parables of the reign of God; the stilling of the storm; the demoniac at

Gerasa; the raising of Jairus' daughter; refused in his own synagogue; sending out the Twelve; John the Baptist put to death; the feeding of the five thousand; the stilling of the storm; clean and unclean food; the little girl with the demon; the deaf and dumb man cured; the feeding of the four thousand; the Pharisees demand a sign; the blind man of Bethsaida; Peter recognizes Jesus as the Christ, but immediately afterward reproves him; the Transfiguration; the epileptic boy; Jesus foretells his death and Resurrection; humility and forgiveness; divorce forbidden; children blessed; the rich young ruler; the Crucifixion foretold; the ambition of James and John; the blind beggar at Jericho; the Triumphal Entry; a fig tree cursed; the Temple cleansed; the fig tree withered; Jesus' authority challenged; the Parable of the Wicked Tenants; debate with the Pharisees; Jesus' unanswerable question; warning against the scribes; the widow's mite; the approaching destruction of Jerusalem; the plot of the high priests; the anointing of Jesus; the treachery of Judas; the Last Supper; Jesus again foretells his death and Resurrection; the Agony in the Garden; betrayal and arrest; the Jewish trial; the Roman trial; the Crucifixion and burial; the Resurrection morning. Each phrase brings a familiar scene to the reader's mind. To such an extent have Peter's recollections of Jesus possessed our memories. Can we say as much for any other apostle or evangelist?

For Peter in the exigencies of primitive Christianity unconsciously filled both roles, to the inexpressible benefit of mankind! In a very real sense and to a considerable extent, Mark embodies what was best in the sermons of Peter, and has there ever been anything like them? You will say, Of course not! He was simply repeating Jesus and telling his story. But how wonderful to be willing and able to tell it with so little loss and alteration. Matthew gave us Jesus' message more fully, and how greatly we prize it, but Mark's story remains supreme, little if at all colored by changing times and circumstances.

For us, certainly Peter's great monument is his Gospel record, not only for what it is and has so long been in itself, but almost more for what it gave to later Evangelists, Matthew and Luke, to give structural soundness to their more ambitious Gospels. Yet could anything done for Christianity ever equal, much less surpass, the creation of the Gospel as a type of literature which gives the Christian faith one of its highest distinctions—the possession of the Gospel as a literary type, the most potent and effective form of religious literature ever developed.

So while Peter wrote nothing, with his preaching he unconsciously set in motion forces of really the utmost consequence. His spoken recollections of Jesus and his words and deeds led swiftly to the writing of the Gospels, first of Mark, then ten years later of Matthew, which Renan called the most important book in the world; then of Luke along with Acts, and then of John. The importance and value of these books to the world's life cannot be estimated. They were also the beginnings of Christian literature, which has so largely colored and purified the literature of the world, far beyond the definite bounds of Christian churches. While Paul, and after him John, have for centuries so largely shaped or at least directed Christian theology, the Gospels of Mark and then of Matthew were the first *books* of Christian literature, and introduced into it those ideas of Jesus from which it can never wholly depart. So even though Peter never wrote a book, he put into his preaching of the gospel memories that soon made one, and launched the prodigious and ever growing stream of Christian literature. So stupendous was the effect of Peter's life and death, and Peter's preaching! No wonder men still consider him the chief of the apostles.

The First Written Gospel

The mood of first-century Judaism was definitely non-literary; it had no mind for writing books. The Qumran scrolls thus far reported do little to interfere with this impression. They are intended simply for the inmates or members of the group—Essenes, or very like them, as careful writers on the scrolls have perceived. There was absolutely no urge to world-wide propaganda. The Covenanters of Qumran were busy realizing themselves and absorbed in the task. They were like the Self-realization Fellowship groups we know in Los Angeles today. Such Hebrew books as the Covenanters produced were concerned with such ideals and outlooks. Even their language reflected their esoteric character; the general public did not know Hebrew, but Aramaic. The Book of Enoch actually states, 69:8-10, that the fourth of the fallen angels to whom Enoch was sent to try to rouse them to repentance was Penemue— "He instructed mankind in writing with ink and paper; and thereby many sinned from eternity to eternity and until this day. For men were not created for such a purpose, to give confirmation to their good faith with pen and ink."

When the Christian movement made its way into the Greek world it awoke to the tremendous value of written books, such as the Greeks reveled in and then produced in such abundance in all sorts of fields—science, medicine, education, rhetoric, criticism, theology, religion—right in the midst of the first century! Every large private house had its library room; one destroyed in Herculaneum in A.D. 79 contained eight hundred scrolls! It was into such a world of

books, authors and publishers that the Christian faith was
just entering; what would its attitude be?

In a fragment of the *Interpretations* of Papias of Hierapolis, fortunately preserved by Eusebius in his *Church
History*, iii:39:15, we read:

> Mark having become the interpreter of Peter, wrote down
> accurately everything that he remembered, without however
> recording in order what was either said or done by Christ. . . .
> So then Mark made no mistake while he thus wrote some things
> as he remembered them, for he made it his one care not to omit
> anything that he heard or to set down any false statement therein.

This is evidently a picture of Mark in Rome after Paul's
death, and Peter's arrival there, and thus ties in with the reference to Mark in Colossians, where, in 4:10, Paul speaks of
him as Barnabas' cousin Mark and adds, "If he comes to see
you, make him welcome." But earlier glimpses of Mark are
afforded by the Acts, where Mark is first mentioned as the
son of a certain Mary, at whose house the church or a part
of it used to meet, Acts 12:12. When Barnabas and Paul
brought the Antioch collection for the needy believers to
Jerusalem, in A.D. 46-47, they took this young man named
John, but also called by his name of Mark (Marcus), back
with them to Antioch. When not long after they set forth on
the First Missionary Journey to the Greek west, they took
John along as their assistant. When Paul had his attack of
coastal fever at Perga, Mark for some unexplained reason
abruptly left the party and returned to Jerusalem, and as
Paul had just come down with a very prostrating illness he
naturally regarded this as a desertion of him at a critical
time. So a couple of years later when he and Barnabas were
planning a second missionary journey, he refused the suggestion of Barnabas that they should again take Mark, Acts
15:37. As the Acts pointedly puts it, Paul did not approve of

taking with them a man who had deserted them in Pamphylia instead of going on with them to their work. "They differed so sharply about it that they separated, and Barnabas took Mark and sailed for Cyprus." That was in A.D. 49. But ten or eleven years later when Paul writes Colossians and Philemon, Mark is one of his fellow workers, Philemon 24. This was no long time before Paul's death, and perhaps three or four years later Peter reaches Rome and finds Mark available as an interpreter, as Peter preached in Aramaic to the Roman Christians. Mark's command of both Greek and Aramaic equipped him admirably for Peter's uses; Paul had needed no interpreter, for he was at home in Greek as well as his native Aramaic.

The invention and general introduction of the leaf-book, the codex, in place of the far less capacious scroll was so opportune for Christian purposes (for Christians wished to make the Jewish Scriptures in the Greek translation available to believers) that some very distinguished scholars have inclined to the view that the codex was a Christian invention for the promotion of their huge religious literature. In old-fashioned Greek scrolls the numerous books of the Old Testament would require thirty or forty scrolls at least; it was for such convenient sizes that the makers of the Greek version of the Old Testament had divided the Mosaic Torah into five convenient Greek scrolls, which the Greeks named Genesis, Exodus, Leviticus, Numbers, Deuteronomy. The Jews, of course, continued to treat them as one scroll, the Torah, seventy or eighty feet long! But how inconvenient, you say! But the Jews seem to have cared nothing for inconvenience.

When the Christians began to publish, with the remembered utterances of the martyred Peter, so soon after his death embodied (about A.D. 70) in our Gospel of Mark, that powerful document led shortly, probably at Antioch, to the Gospel of Matthew, which embodied substantially all of

Mark, but immeasurably enriched it with the remembered sayings and even discourses of Jesus. This was probably about A.D. 80. Ten years later the publication of Luke's two-volume work we know as Luke and Acts, awakened great interest in the works of Paul and someone at Colossae or Laodicea had a couple of letters from him, preserved in those churches. If he preached in all the places mentioned in the Acts, who knew what letters from him they might possess, filed away in their church chests? The result of such inquiries was the collection of Paul's ten letters, published soon after, probably at Ephesus. Up to that time no Christian writer had shown any literary influence of Paul; but from then on to the present day, every Christian writer has shown it! You see how the Christian entry into literature, and the publication of Christian writing was accelerating!

But observe the climax! For probably early in the second century, at Ephesus, where Paul's letters had so recently appeared, Christian publishers put together all four of the Greek Gospels, Matthew, Mark, Luke and the new Gospel of John, arranged from the most Jewish to the most Greek and achieved a publishing success that has never been surpassed! The Gospels were now shown to be not rivals but allies, and no publishing success has ever rivaled this. The four Gospels! Does the world contain their equal? In power? In depth? In influence? We take them for granted, but some great spirits in Ephesus saw that they were to be understood together, not separately, and put them together. This was no matter of course; most people would have thought their differences would confuse more than they helped and have chosen one and dropped the rest. But not these great publishers of Ephesus who gave us, for our eternal welfare, the Fourfold Gospel.

They became very popular—and see them today, much the most beloved and influential and most published of all

the books of the Bible. Certainly the publishers who collected them and gave them to the churches were no less
than inspired! This, we repeat, was not an act of writing or
editing or revising, but of publishing, pure and simple, and
it was an act that worlds of readers, then unborn and un-
dreamed of, have not outgrown. The Bible societies tell us
that the four Gospels are the parts of the Bible most read
and most in demand. We cannot learn that it was ordered
by any council—there were no church councils as yet—or
by any church. A Christian publisher or a group of them
under the aegis of the great church at Ephesus, the greatest
of Paul's foundations, in an inspired moment saw the supreme value in the four *together* and set them on their way.
And they have never faltered. What a glimpse of church life
in the early years of the second century—by A.D. 120.

A few years ago a young scholar, C. H. Roberts, at Man-
chester found in a mass of broken scraps of Greek papyri a
tiny bit with a few words from John *on each side!* That
meant it was from a leaf-book, a codex, and the handwriting
the best learning has ascribed to the reign of Hadrian, A.D.
117-138. Christian publishers were already using the leaf-
book, so universal today, in the circulation of the Greek
gospels, around 130-140! I am reminded that in my student
days I went into a native bookstore in Damascus and asked
for a copy of the Koran, in Arabic. The clerk asked me if I
was a Moslem, and I said No, I was a Christian. He said he
could not sell me a Koran. A few weeks later, in the Fayum,
in Egypt, I went into a native bookstore in Medinet and asked
for a Koran, with the same result! It was the prescribed
Moslem attitude; no Korans for unbelievers! I admit my
purpose was not very serious; I had a perfectly good Koran
in Arabic at home, in Chicago. But the incident does set the
Christian attitude in strong relief.

While Christian tradition has long connected Mark's later

years with the mission to Egypt, especially Alexandria, the oldest historical materials give no support to such a ministry, welcome as it would be in explaining the origin of Christianity in Alexandria, half a century later such a significant center of Christian life and education. Both Greek and Coptic Christianity were extremely active in Egypt from early in the second century.

The Gospel According to Matthew

The ancient and long cherished view that Matthew the Apostle was the author of the Gospel that bears his name has in modern times been generally relinquished by scholars, because it makes so much use of Mark's Gospel and other apparent written sources. Yet equally serious considerations may lead us to return to it. Jesus' purpose in gathering a group of intimate disciples had its background in the case of Isaiah, who after a notable work as a prophet was put to death by the king who resented him. Yet no prophet did more than he, for his disciples preserved his messages, and when the skies cleared made them known; indeed, they virtually published them to the nation. Jesus' repeated references to Isaiah and his writings show his regard for him and them. In particular, his calling twelve disciples to join him and virtually live with him repeats the course Isaiah had taken, which in his case was all that had rescued his work from oblivion. Jesus was no less farseeing; the case of John the Baptist's work and fate was right before his eyes. This is why Jesus chooses an inner circle of disciples whose duty it shall be to carry on his work if he too is cut short. That he should leave this tremendous responsibility to a group of earnest fishermen is hardly probable. Was there no one in his circle who might rise to the writer's task, as Isaiah's disciples had so nobly done? Jesus was very much alive to the Book of Isaiah; did he have no such idea for his own message? Isaiah had said, "I will bind up my testimony, and seal my teaching in the heart of my disciples. Then I will wait for the Lord." Isa. 8:16, 17.

Jesus may well have had his eyes open for one disciple who could in a measure record his message, short though the time might be before the end! In Matthew the tax collector may he not have found such a possible recorder? More is made of his call in all three of the earliest Gospels than of that of any one of the Twelve. The Evangelist Mark, reflecting Peter's recollections, shows that Matthew's call had struck the disciples as an event. His social position, his profession, so distasteful to orthodox Judaism, his business—all made him a striking figure among the Twelve—richer, better educated, accustomed to the ways of the world. His first act was to celebrate his new connection with a dinner, Luke says, for his friends and associates to meet his new Master, for he is to be one of his disciples! Surely this is not putting too much into an event so carefully recorded by Matthew, Mark and Luke, all three. Matthew even takes care not to name this disciple Levi, as Mark and Luke did, but Matthew.

Some scholars hold that Jesus gave the dinner in his, that is Peter's, house, Mark 2:15 (or some say in a house of his own!), including many tax collectors among those present. Matthew seems to understand it in that way. But if Jesus so promptly gave such a dinner in Peter's house (or a house of his own) after calling Matthew, and evidently including him, it would signalize his call even more than if, as Luke understands, Matthew gave it. In Mark's narrative, Matthew is the fifth individual called to follow Jesus; he had called Peter, Andrew, James and John, immediately on reaching the lake, to follow him as his disciples. It is reasonable to suppose that in following Jesus, Matthew must have given up his tax-collecting profession.

Let us note the beginning of his Gospel, so dependent for most of its *action* upon Mark! A genealogy of Jesus, from the patriarch Abraham, through David and the kings of Judah, through the Exile and Return, all carefully grouped in three fourteens! But why? To point out not too flatly, that Jesus begins a seventh seven! What a numerical climax! And he is a climax! But what kind of a writer is this, that presents his opening emphasis so veiled in a succession of statistics? Well, perhaps he *is* a statistician, by taste and experience, and no other than our old friend Matthew! Can a more probable explanation of this extraordinary approach be proposed? Could we ask a more convincing sign-manual of the Man of Figures? He names himself the author, not bluntly but with Jewish ambiguity; the understanding will understand!

For to Matthew, an old man at Antioch, where the Jerusalem Christians had gone after the fall of Jerusalem, soon after comes the Gospel of Mark! What a splendid effort at a great task! But so weak in Jesus' teaching! The tragedy and the drama are there, but not the incomparable treasure of his instruction! That must go in! And Matthew is the man to incorporate it. And how obscure Mark's approach! That must be remedied! And how massively Matthew did it! The genealogy, for Jewish readers; the Magi and the Star would reach and fascinate the great religious public who believed in astrology; and the Virgin Birth will arrest the Stoic section of the religious public who explained every supremely great man as a son of God, that is Zeus, by special generation!

Here was an introduction to the whole religious public of the Greco-Roman world sufficiently elevated to be at all accessible to the Gospel. Then, best of all, Jesus' *teaching* in something like its fulness. So out of Mark's moving *narrative* came Matthew's larger presentation of Jesus the

Teacher, making his Gospel what Renan a century ago called the most important book in the world.

It is notable that Matthew's call is almost the only one in Mark so individualized. Jesus calls Simon and Andrew, together; they are to catch men! Nothing is said about the individual calling of most of the Twelve. Only Matthew is individualized. He is called from his bookkeeping and his accounts, but of course the old bookkeeper is just the man to work up the genealogy through the royal line, from the historical books of the Old Testament, making Jesus begin the seventh seven, and he is just the man to be interested in the astronomical coincidence with the birth of Jesus, and the use the astrologers made of it; and to be aware of Herod's ways and death, and his successors. Such things mattered to a tax collector.

This is not proof, but it must be admitted that if the author was not Matthew the tax-collector apostle, he must have been someone very much like him. He is also well aware of Greco-Roman Stoicism, with its Zeus-descended heroes, which forms the background of the Virgin Birth record. Could a Capernaum tax collector have known all these things? Yes, he if anybody in that area, and certainly, after some years amid the idolatry of Antioch. He is a man of the world, but with a religious interest to which Jesus strongly appealed. And in his old age, for he must have been seventy or eighty years of age when he wrote his great book, he begins it with an appeal to Jews, astrologers and Stoics— the great faiths of the hour.

We must also remember that in the Greek world in which the Gospels arose, people cared about authorship, as Judaism never did. As Eduard Meyer used to say, oriental literature was prevailingly anonymous; the Hebrew prophets rise like islands in a sea of anonymity! But if you wrote in Greek, people expected the author to be named. The writers of the Gospels were named; Mark, Luke, John rightly enough—and why not Matthew? He was no great figure to be invoked to give prestige to a book—unless he was the man who wrote it! The authorship of the Gospel of Matthew must be studied in the light of all these considerations.

It is usually assumed that Matthew the Apostle would not have used what others had previously written on the subject, if he had written a Gospel. On the other hand, he lived in his later life, we may assume, in Antioch, to which city the Christians of Jerusalem moved when Jerusalem was threatened by the Romans, in the war of A.D. 66-70. They understood it to be the command of Jesus, Mark 13:14, 15; they were to make the best of their escape to the hills around. If he was the taxgatherer we suppose, and not an instinctively creative writer, he might well take advantage of such partial written accounts of Jesus and his teaching as were available; his purpose was to supply the deficiencies of Mark's Gospel from his knowledge and information. It is no more difficult to imagine Matthew doing this than to imagine some unknown imaginary figure doing so. Matthew, or the author of Matthew, seems to have used two other sources besides Mark which were also afterward used by Luke when he wrote his Gospel volume at Ephesus some ten years later. But about one-seventh of what is contained in Matthew is material found in no other Gospel, and much that Luke also contains, for example the Lord's Prayer, has always seemed to Christian hearts better put, in Matthew; no one uses Luke's Lord's Prayer! Matthew's Gospel had not reached Luke; Antioch was no such center of publication as Ephesus. Moreover, Matthew rearranges much of Mark's sequence of incidents as Luke does not venture to do. And the fulness and force of Jesus' rebuke of Pharisaic legalism and formalism, chapter 13, could find no better reporter than the publican who had

so long suffered under their bitterness and pretended supe-
riority.

The Gospel of Matthew is some seventy pages long; one-
half of it, or thirty-five pages, is plainly derivable—and de-
rived—from Mark. Here was the factual basis of Matthew,
ready to the writer's hand. But he was alive to its defects—
so confused in its approach and so deficient in Jesus' teaching. These things are enough to stir the author to undertake
its rewriting, and that is what Matthew does. Would it be
strange if a man possessed of the Sermon on the Mount and
what we find in Matthew, chapter 25, felt driven to make
of Mark the greater book that it suggests? We may remember that in the history of literature one book constantly
suggests another, and not infrequently a good book will sug-
gest a better one that can be written. So the occasion of
Matthew is the arrival at Antioch of the Gospel of Mark.

Almost every action or event in Matthew is to be found—
and Matthew probably found it—in the Gospel of Mark; the
story of Jesus, the Man of Action. The characteristic feature
of Matthew's Gospel is its great discourses; it does not add
greatly to our knowledge of what Jesus did, but so much to
our knowledge of what he said, especially in his great sermons. But they are precisely the characteristic feature of
Matthew. While incorporating into his Gospel most of what
Mark recorded in the way of action, Matthew makes of most
of it simply the frame of Jesus' great sermons. After the
perils of his infancy and childhood, his baptism and temptation, Matthew's Gospel is almost a collection of Jesus' sermons; first the Sermon of the Mount, chapters 5, 6 and 7,
setting forth the ethical ideals of the Kingdom of Heaven.
This comes as near being the Constitution of the Christian
Church as anything in the Bible. Matthew boldly challenges
comparison of it with the Ten Commandments by describing
Jesus as going up on a mountain to utter it. And what had

he to offer mankind to compare with them? Matthew's tremendous answer is, The Sermon on the Mount! You feel
yourself in the presence of an Evangelist who is a master of
great drama! Is Jesus, then, greater than Moses? Of course
he is!

We begin to wonder at this wealth of teaching material,
forty or fifty years after the Crucifixion! Did Matthew remember all this? The sermons that follow, for after a couple
of chapters, 8 and 9, of incident mostly drawn from Mark,
Matthew goes right on with another sermon, chapter 10, on
the Proclamation of the Kingdom, uttered at the sending out
of the Twelve. Again he returns to Mark's narrative for chapters 11 and 12, for a series of incidents, introducing the third
sermon, 13:1-52, on the Growth and Worth of the Kingdom.
The disciples now recognize Jesus as the Messiah of Jewish
expectation, but he foresees his own death. In a fourth sermon, chapter 18, Jesus tells of life in the Kingdom. Then in
Jerusalem, challenged by the Jewish leaders, he utters the
terrific Parable of the Wicked Tenants, pronouncing the
doom of the city and nation. This is the turning point of the
action. They had refused the Kingdom of God, and whoever
that stone falls upon will be pulverized! Matthew did not
overestimate the blow that had befallen them.

In a fifth discourse Jesus denounces the religious leaders
who had so misled the Jews, chapter 23. Then follows the
sixth and final sermon, the fall of Jerusalem and the End of
the Age, chapters 24 and 25, ending in the climax of Jesus'
teaching, the Parable of the Last Judgment! What a record
of Jesus' preaching! No less a man could have done it! Was
it Matthew the Apostle who had listened so closely and remembered (or recorded) so faithfully? Had he depended
solely upon his close attention and his memory? Or had he
taken notes, like a Greek, but unlike a Jew (unless he was a
tax collector, whose profession was to make notes), and re-

corded what he heard from time to time? We cannot say. But what he wrote down has very largely mastered the Christian consciousness ever since.

Certainly Jesus made no mistake in selecting Peter as his first apostle, and if, as tradition declares, Matthew is the writer of the Gospel that bears his name, Jesus made no mistake in choosing him. Whatever doubts or difficulties may beset us as to its authorship, no more probable author of it can be suggested. Indeed, it is hard to see why the name of an otherwise obscure figure like Matthew the tax collector should ever have been given it, unless he was identified with its origin.

8

THE MISSION FIELDS OF THE APOSTLES

EUSEBIUS does not hesitate to tell at the beginning of the third book of his great *Church History* what were the individual fields of labor assigned to the several apostles. "Parthia, according to tradition," he says, "was allotted to Thomas as his field of labor; Scythia, to Andrew, and Asia to John, who after he had lived some time there, died at Ephesus. Peter appears to have preached in Pontus, Galatia, Bithynia, Cappadocia and Asia [names suggested by I Peter 1:1], to the Jews of the Dispersion, and at last, having come to Rome he was crucified head downwards, for he had requested that he might suffer in this way."

Here Eusebius drops the subject of the twelve apostles, turning to the labors of Paul, with which he was a good deal more familiar.

This leaves eight apostles with their fields of labor unaccounted for, even by Eusebius. Has ancient literature or tradition nothing to say of them? Not that it possessed all the facts as to their work. We know full well that Christianity did spread in an amazing way through the Roman Empire and beyond its limits; the Jews had long been indefatigable missionaries, Matt. 23:15. The gospel had reached Damascus very early; Paul (as Saul) about A.D. 34-35 was sent there to suppress it! It had reached Rome before A.D. 56, when there was a flourishing church there, to which Paul wrote perhaps his greatest letter. It also reached Alexandria early, though we know little about its beginnings there; the Roman dread of race riots there must have hampered its beginnings in Egypt. Who first carried the gospel in all directions, as was so evidently done? That is what the twelve apostles were told to do. Matt. 28:19, 20, and it is reasonable to suppose that they were among the leaders in doing it. Indeed, many old church traditions support apostolic responsibility in their foundation. We must remember that few of the early missions found historians, as Paul's did in his beloved doctor, Luke, Col. 4:14.

It is interesting to survey the traditions of these apostolic missions that still persist in far-off lands. As I write these lines my cousin, Miss Helen Hunt, long dean of women at Judson College, Rangoon, Burma, tells me of the Mar Thoma (Syriac for St. Thomas) Church of South India, a recognized part of the Syrian Orthodox Church. Outside of Madras is a hill which is called St. Thomas Mount. It is the strong belief of this group, she informs me, that their church was founded by St. Thomas during the first century, and that he was in South India personally. This group of Christians is probably the best known, and one of the largest, if not the largest and most highly respected in India. They are not coolies, but people of education. Their home is in Travancore State.

If we compare this tradition of the mission field of Thomas, we observe that Eusebius says he went to Parthia, and Parthia we are told, since splitting off from Persia in the third century B.C., had grown into a vast empire, extending from the Euphrates to the Indus—that is, to the borders of India. It is true Madras is far from the Indus, being on the east coast of the great peninsula, but what is a thousand

miles to an expanding religion, especially in well-nigh two
thousand years? Here is a surviving and flourishing Christianity claiming its foundation by Thomas, nineteen centuries
ago.

Some scholars maintain that the Thomas who founded this
Christian group in India was not the apostle but a later
Nestorian missionary; the name, it is maintained, cannot be
traced back further than the eighth century. Yet at least the
projected influence of Thomas seems to be reflected in it, if,
as seems probable, Parthia was his province.

In what is said to be the oldest form of the tradition about
the missionary apportionments made to the apostles, the
Black Sea region was assigned to Peter, Andrew, Matthew
and Bartholomew; Parthia, to Thomas, Thaddeus and
"Simeon the Canaanite" (Zealot); and Asia Minor to John
and Philip. But this distribution breaks down at a number
of points.

The Black Sea lands, that is, the lands fronting on the
Black Sea, would naturally be Thrace, Bithynia, Pontus and
Armenia. The assignment of Parthia to Thomas is sound
enough, as we have seen. But apportioning Bithynia and
Pontus to Peter can only be due to the address of First Peter
to "those who are scattered as foreigners over Pontus, Galatia, Cappadocia, Asia and Bithynia," a letter written from the
Roman church long after the lifetime of Peter and designed
to offset and counteract the dangerous and almost rebellious
attitude of the Revelation, which had so recently reached
those districts. Galatia and Asia were emphatically in Paul's
missionary orbit; he had evangelized them. First Peter addresses these regions because they are neighbors of the
seven churches of Asia addressed in Rev. 1:11, and more fully
in its first three chapters. There is no reason to believe that
they were included in the personal ministry of Peter. It is

quite true that John, the writer of the Revelation, preached in Ephesus toward the end of the first century, as did John the Evangelist a few years later still. Yet on the whole this oldest tradition of missionary assignment seems far from historical.

As for Armenia, the Armenian tradition is that Thaddeus and Bartholomew evangelized that country, which is interesting since these two names are not paired in any of our New Testament lists; in Matthew, it is Philip and Bartholomew that form the third pair, while Thaddeus stands second in the fifth pair, with the second James. Mark does not give the apostles in pairs, but Bartholomew is sixth and Thaddeus tenth. Luke puts Bartholomew sixth in his Gospel, seventh in Acts, where he is paired with Matthew; he does not mention Thaddeus in either list, calling him Judas son of James.

It is a striking fact that the so-called Acts of Thomas relate the mission of Thomas to India, and they were written early in the third century, as modern authorities (Harnack, M. R. James) agree. This goes far to confirm the legend of the Syrian Indian church, that Thomas did indeed not only cross Parthia with his message but actually penetrated India with it! These Acts have some links with the first-century Indian history, also. Yet we must also remember that "India" was a term very loosely used by the ancients, as the statement that Bartholomew went there as a missionary and found "the Gospel of Matthew in Hebrew" shows. Eusebius declares, in his *Church History*, v:10:2, that about the time of the accession of Commodus, A.D. 180, Pantaenus, the leading teacher in the church at Alexandria, was sent as missionary as far as India. He goes on to say that Bartholomew had preached to them, and left with them the Gospel of Matthew "in the Hebrew language," a very perplexing statement! Indeed, it is sometimes said that "India" in the first century was very loosely used, being understood to begin on the Bosporus. Alexander's march to India had done much three and a half centuries before the Christian mission began, toward opening the great Parthian hinterland to the western mind. He had reached the easternmost of the tributaries of the Indus River before he turned south to the Indian Ocean and then west again. His great march and the seventy cities he had built or founded had in a measure opened the way to India.

Armenian tradition, Miss Louise Nalbandian tells me, names four other apostles besides Thaddeus and Bartholomew who preached the gospel in Armenia—Simon the Canaanite (meaning the Cananaean or Zealot, of Matt. 10:4; Mark 3:18); Judas (meaning Judas son of James, Acts 1:13, who is usually identified with Thaddeus of Mark 3:18; Matt. 10:3); Andrew; and Matthias, the thirteenth apostle, appointed to take the place of Judas Iscariot, Acts 1:26. Allowing for these identifications, the total list of apostolic missionaries to Armenia would number five—Thaddeus, Bartholomew, Simon the Zealot, Andrew, and Matthias. Origen, as quoted by Eusebius, says that Andrew was to evangelize Scythia, the region north and northeast of the Black Sea, and if so his district would lie directly north of Armenia, but separated from it by the Caucasus Mountains!

In his *Church History* Eusebius records that about A.D. 250 Dionysius of Alexandria wrote a letter to the brethren of Armenia, where Merozanes was bishop. In his interesting book on the *Mission and Expansion of Christianity in the First Three Centuries,* Harnack includes the western part of Armenia among the lands most Christianized by A.D. 325; it had indeed officially accepted the gospel in 301.

It is the Armenian tradition that Thaddeus and Bartholomew even translated the Scriptures into Armenian, though of course little of the New Testament had in their time been published or written. They may have introduced the Armenian version of the Old Testament, or more probably leading parts of it, into Armenian. It is now generally held that the New Testament was not put into Armenian until A.D. 400 (when Mesrop devised or improved the Armenian alphabet), being then first translated from the Syriac version. The fuller Old Testament was doubtless later translated into Armenian.

To Andrew, tradition has assigned Scythia, north of the Black Sea, as his mission field, but the Acts of Andrew, written probably about A.D. 260, describes his labors as taking place chiefly in Greece or in Macedonia, where his martyrdom occurs at Patras (Patrae) as described in his *Acts*.

The connection of John with Asia, that is western Asia Minor, as his mission field, with its chief center at Ephesus, must arise from the identification of John the Apostle with John the Prophet of the Revelation, Rev. 1:2, about A.D. 95, or with John the Evangelist, about 110, both of whom were Ephesian figures. The original evangelization of Ephesus, however, and of the Asia interior was clearly the work of Paul and his circle, as described in Acts, chapter 19. Indeed, this church turned out to be Paul's most significant and influential foundation in the generation that followed.

We must not suppose that any apostle necessarily confined his labors to a single district or even country. They must have made much use of interpreters, as Peter did in Rome, and have moved from place to place and from one country to another, as opportunities arose. Whatever assignment of definite fields of labor they made must have been subject to subsequent developments; the story of Paul's missionary movements in Asia Minor and Greece shows that.

Egypt was practically closed to the Christian mission by

reason of the Romans' dread of race riots there, if some pro-
vocative Jewish figure appeared on the scene, and such
people were virtually excluded. This was undoubtedly why
the Early Church undertook no active Egyptian mission that
we know of in New Testament times. Tradition, however, has
filled this gap with the legend or tradition of Mark and his
ministry in Alexandria. But Mark was, of course, not an
apostle but what we may call a subapostolic figure.

PART TWO
Apostolic Sequels

9

THE LETTERS OF THE APOSTLES

First Peter

ROUND the names of some of the apostles—Peter, James, John, Jude—there gathered a few letters written in their names, evidently under the influence of the great collection of Paul's letters. Paul's letters were collected and published soon after the appearance, about A.D. 90, of Luke's two-volume work which we know as the Gospel of Luke and the Acts of the Apostles. In the years that followed, two devoted adherents of Peter put forth letters in his name, designed to meet the problems of the time, in accord with what they believed was his spirit and attitude. They did this with no intention of deceiving their readers, who understood well enough that Peter was not their actual author. For one thing, they felt so thoroughly identified with Peter in spirit and doctrine that they could properly speak in his name; for another, the book of Revelation had just appeared and one aspect of its message, it seemed to them, must be corrected at once, as they believed Peter would have wished it corrected.

The eloquent letter known to us as Hebrews had just made its appearance and expressly called upon the church at Rome to live up to its role of teaching and leading the churches; its age if nothing else demanded this: "For although from the length of your Christian experience you ought to be teaching others, you actually need someone to teach you over again the very elements of Christian truth!" The duty of the Roman recipients of Hebrews could hardly be put more strongly. Certainly the Roman church responded promptly and vigorously to this challenge, for First Peter is certainly a letter from the Roman church—"your sister-church in Babylon," as Revelation and other Jewish and early Christian writers called Rome, I Peter 5:13. First Peter boldly corrected the almost rebellious attitude to the Roman Empire which the book of Revelation had taken, which if adopted by the churches in general would have brought the church and the empire into downright war with each other. Revelation had been painstakingly addressed to no less than seven churches of the province of Asia, scattered all the way from Ephesus to Laodicea. But their influence would reach on, northward, to the churches not only of Asia but of Pontus, Galatia, Cappadocia and Bithynia—all northern and interior Asia Minor and the Christians of these districts. The Roman church, roused to its responsibility by Hebrews, now makes a noble effort to save them from adopting a rebellious attitude toward Rome. That would have done the Christian cause no good, but on the contrary would have led to prompt efforts at its extinction by Rome.

So in I Peter the church at Rome takes up its task and burden of teaching and guiding the other churches. This it does, not unnaturally, in the name of its great martyr-leader Peter. In a time of persecution, felt among all the churches, 5:9, it gives sound Christian counsel to these northern churches: they are to submit to the emperor, not rebel against him, 2:13-17; and not be surprised if persecution comes their way, 4:12-19. We may therefore think of this message of I Peter as called forth by the stinging words addressed to Rome in Heb. 5:12 to 6:2.

First Peter is in excellent Greek, such Greek as Peter himself could not have written, if he had to preach to the Greek-speaking audiences at Rome in Aramaic and be translated sentence by sentence by his interpreters. But it is in his name, for he had made the Roman church his, by his preaching and his martyrdom, and it afterward made him its patron saint, or one of them, for it still writes in the names of Peter and Paul. We must remember that some of the ancients thought it was the truest devotion to a revered leader to write in his name what they felt would be his message for the hour and the emergency that were upon them. Especially in the pressing situation created by the Revelation of John—which threatened to turn the Christian believers into bitter rebels against the Roman Empire, when as a matter of fact they were the best citizens it had except for this one matter of paganism, particularly emperor worship—the Roman Christians felt entitled to speak in the name of the Apostle Peter himself to stem the tide.

But now, thirty or thirty-five years have passed since the death of Peter. The chief of the apostles had been suddenly snatched away at the height of his usefulness and hurried to a martyr's death. The legend is that as he was to be crucified, he protested that it must be head downward, as he was not worthy to die as Jesus had died. Tradition also has it that Peter was fleeing from Rome to escape arrest and death when he met Jesus coming into the city. Peter cried out in amazement,

"Master, where are you going?" (*Domine, quo vadis?*) and Jesus replied,

"Into the city, to be crucified again!"

And Peter turned back, to arrest and martyrdom.[1] Those

[1] Acts of Peter, ch. 35.

were the dreadful days of Nero, whose hideous cruelties to the Christians of Rome stirred even pagan writers to horror and pity. Tacitus, the Roman historian of half a century later, in the fifteenth book of his *Annals*, wrote of the burning of Rome how Nero charged it to the Christians, and says:

> Accordingly first those were seized who confessed they were Christians, next, on their information, a vast multitude were convicted, not so much on the charge of burning the city as of hating the human race. And in their deaths they were also made the subjects of sport, for they were covered with the hides of wild beasts, and worried to death by dogs, or nailed to crosses, or set fire to, and when day declined burned to serve for nocturnal lights. Nero offered his own gardens for the spectacle.

If one can look past the horror of this almost contemporary pagan account of the attack, one observes that already there were a host of Christian believers in Rome itself. And if Peter had already reached Rome by 64 he can hardly have escaped this persecution.

That Peter did reach Rome the New Testament itself strongly suggests. I Peter 5:13 speaks on behalf of "your sister-church in Babylon," as though the writer, ostensibly Peter, were in Rome. For it is a well-known fact that in such books as Baruch, the Letter of Jeremiah, II Esdras and the Revelation, Rome is habitually referred to as Babylon, the traditional oppressor of the Hebrews. Especially in I Peter, written in answer to the Revelation, it is perfectly natural to speak of Rome in the figurative language the Revelation had just used. That the Revelation uses Babylon of Rome is made transparently clear when the author of it, John of Ephesus, describes the city of Babylon as seated on seven hills, 17:9. Of course this transports the reader at once to Rome, so long famed as built upon seven hills.

The following statement that "Mark my son . . . wishes to

be remembered to you" can only mean that Paul's young friend Mark had become a sort of secretary of Peter, and points to his presence with Paul at Rome in his final imprisonment, Col. 4:10; Philemon 24. Our oldest Gospel bears the name of Mark, but at the same time in it after the first page we are so constantly in the presence, the house, the boat of Peter that the impression that he is the main voucher—even the chief source—of the story becomes irresistible. What, then, had Mark to do with it? The ancient tradition preserved in our fragments of Papias of Hierapolis, about A.D. 140, is that when Peter came to Rome and preached to the eager Christians there in his native Aramaic, Mark was one of those who stood beside him and sentence by sentence translated his utterances into Greek; the Roman church we remember was a Greek-speaking church almost to the middle of the third century! Hearing Peter tell these precious stories of the doings and sayings of Jesus and repeating them after him, in Greek, naturally fixed them in the mind and memory of Mark. When Peter, the source of them, was suddenly snatched away from the Roman church and hurried to a fearful death, the sense of all they had lost in the death of their sole direct link with Jesus as he had lived and talked in Galilee, must have made Peter's death doubly desolating. Until this young Jew, who knew Greek so well, took his pen and wrote down what he remembered of all that Peter had told of Jesus' doings and teachings, and the terrible story of his arrest and trial and death—and return. Those two chapters, 14, 15, are high tragedy indeed, none higher in all literature, and they owe their power to no man's art, but to the sheer awful pathos of what they tell. They strike the deep note of reality, that there's no gainsaying. The later Evangelists followed them, but did not overtake them.

This is why the writer of First Peter, years after, made Peter call him affectionately "Mark my son!" He had done more than a son's part for the heroic apostle. Which makes us understand Peter's prominence in this earliest Gospel; he was not its author, but he was its source. It became the chief source for the narrative, the action of the later Gospels of Matthew and Luke. As already said, I have found fourteen-fifteenths of Mark repeated (with much besides!) in Matthew. But my long-ago friend Canon Streeter of Oxford said he found nineteen-twentieths of Mark taken over into Matthew! Matthew incorporated virtually all of Mark into his Gospel. Even Luke has taken over three-fifths of it into his. So Mark did a prodigious service in recording Peter's memories of Jesus and his teaching, for his work strongly colors all three of the first-century Gospels, which are the very foundation of Christian thought and action. While Paul's letters were written before Mark wrote his Gospel, Mark's Gospel was published and circulating widely among the churches of the first century twenty years before Paul's letters were collected and published. We must remember that the Greeks and Romans of that time were no strangers to the art of publication, even though their books had to be written by hand. But slave labor, sometimes of the utmost skill, enabled one Roman poet of the first century to get out a book every year; every fine house had its library room, and the great cities like Alexandria had magnificent large libraries containing hundreds of thousands of scrolls. Indeed, the handwriting of those slave-scribes has given the models to the type designers of our own day.

The first century was an age of book writing, Greek and Latin, and of book publishing on a surprising scale, and into that world Greek Christians entered by about A.D. 70 with Peter's memories of the words and work of Jesus, recorded after Peter's death by his faithful Greek-speaking interpreter Mark. This book had at once a great effect and influence. It was nothing less than the beginning of Christian literature. It became the core of the quartette of Gospels put together by Christian publishers about A.D. 120-125 which has been the most brilliant success in the whole history of book publication, and is so still!

We find the reflection of Paul's letters on every page of I Peter, and for the Revelation's attitude to persecution, I Peter substitutes a far nobler one, reviving Paul's position of loyalty to what was best in the Roman Empire, Rom. 13:1-7. I Peter reflects one letter of Paul's after another, II Corinthians, Ephesians, Colossians, Galatians, Romans, and so on.

The purpose of the letter was to use Peter's great prestige to relieve the perilous position into which the Revelation threatened to put the churches, by seeming to make the Christian movement a revolutionary body seeking the overthrow of the Roman Empire.

Second Peter

The second letter under Peter's name shows a very different background. The Docetic sect had arisen in Christian circles, and actually held that the spirit could find fellowship with God, while what the body did really did not very much matter. It saw little spiritual meaning in the death of Jesus, in fact the Docetists felt no particular need of an Atonement.

Against this doctrine a Christian named Jude, probably about A.D. 125, wrote a short, vehement protest and denunciation, warning Christian believers against the Docetists and their ways, their fanciful views and their loose morals. Like Ephesians, it is boldly addressed to Christians everywhere. The writer of II Peter reproduces this invective almost entire in the middle part of his letter, of which it forms much of the second chapter, though in II Peter it is now directed at those who deny the Second Coming, probably about A.D. 160.

The writer of II Peter already has a remarkable Christian library. He shows unmistakable acquaintance with the four Gospels, the letters of Paul, Hebrews, Jude and I Peter, and when he wrote, the Gospels and Paul's ten letters were already being regarded as Scripture. He introduced much of the Letter of Jude little changed into the midst of his argument; it forms substantially what we know as the second chapter of II Peter. II Peter definitely relates itself to I Peter, 3:1: "This is the second letter, dear friends, that I have now written to you." In 1:12-16 the writer refers his readers to the Gospel of Mark, as embodying memories of Jesus, and in 1:15 he even alludes to John 21:19 as a reference to his own crucifixion.

The attitude of the author of I Peter that the church at Rome could speak in the name and with the authority of Peter thus reappears in II Peter, and he feels justified in directing the vigorous invective of the Letter of Jude against the group that was denying the doctrine of the Second Coming of Christ.

James

The most familiar of the seven General Letters is that of James, which constitutes nothing less than a masterpiece of early Christian preaching. It is a fine example of the conversational sermon, from which the "homily"—conversation—took its name. Such a sermon has almost the form of a conversation between the preacher and his auditor. It so often reminds us of Matthew that the author of it must have known that Gospel. He also knew Paul's collected letters, for he discusses a current abuse of their great doctrine of faith. He also shows the use of I Peter and Hebrews.

He wrote probably in the circle of Syrian Antioch, in most excellent Greek. The letter, which must have been a favorite with all Christians almost from the first, was named in honor of James the brother of Jesus, who became such a pillar of the Jerusalem church; Matthew and Mark put him first as clearly the eldest of Jesus' brothers, James, Joseph, Judas and Simon, Mark 6:3; Matt. 13:55. James is already at the head of the church when Peter after his escape from prison calls at the house of Mark's mother and asks them to report his escape from prison to "James and the brothers," Acts 12:17. He seems to rank in standing next to Peter himself. When Paul and Barnabas, after the First Missionary Journey, go down to Jerusalem to discuss the question of demanding circumcision of Gentile converts, Acts, chapter 15, Peter makes a strong appeal, and finally James formulates the compromise that is adopted, vs. 13-21. On Paul's last visit to Jerusalem, he immediately calls upon James, 21:18, and he and the elders give Paul the advice which turned out so disastrously. James does not seem to have realized the importance of the Greek mission or to have been in entire sympathy with it. In I Cor. 15:7 Paul mentions James as one of those who had seen Jesus after the Resurrection, and in Gal. 1:19 Paul mentions seeing only Cephas and James the Lord's brother on his brief visit to Jerusalem, after his return from Damascus. In Gal. 2:9 he speaks of James, with Cephas and John as pillars of the church; who promised Paul and Barnabas their co-operation in their missionary work among the Greeks, though later, v. 12, his emissaries seemed to go back on this promise. Some believe the James mentioned in Jude 1—"the brother of James"—was James of Jerusalem, which would make him also the brother of Jesus himself, but this is improbable. For if he was, why not say so? There was no hesitation in speaking of James as the Lord's brother, Matt. 13:55; Mark 6:3; Gal. 1:19.

It is not easy to find a specific occasion for the letter, it is so fitting and timely in every age and place! Nor is it easy to trace a course of thought in the letter. It consists of a series of moral and religious observations of great pungency and force, but there is no great effort at logical sequence; they are hardly a chain of links, each one suggesting or introducing the next; they are more like beads on a string, or even a handful of pearls! The observations are in the highest degree practical and pointed. Young Christians in particular find James of intense interest and value.

Certainly no nobler tribute could have been paid to James than to give his name to this masterly statement of practical Christianity. Perhaps its apparent contrast with Paul's great emphasis upon faith, James 2:14-26, influenced early Christianity in giving James' name to this short sermon, hardly twenty minutes long.

Jude

The short and vehement letter of Jude was a denunciation, as we have seen, of the Docetists of the early second century, around 125, for the laxity of their morals and their fanciful views. It contains the longest clear quotation from the apocryphal Book of Enoch that was known prior to the discovery of that work in an Ethiopic version, by Bruce in Abyssinia in 1773, Jude 14, 15; Enoch 1:9. Enoch probably took shape gradually in the second and first centuries before Christ.

Just what Jude is referred to as the author cannot be determined. The words "the brother of James" were probably added to the name Judas which we anglicize as Jude. But which James is meant? There was a James who was a brother of Jesus, who held aloof from Jesus during his ministry and even joined in the efforts of his family to prevail upon him to suspend it, Mark 3:21, 31-35. In Mark 6:3 James seems to be the eldest, for he heads the list of the four brothers of Jesus—James, Joses, Judas and Simon. In Gal. 1:19, written in A.D. 52, Paul mentions him as though he were an apostle, and indeed he practically made a place for himself as their chief, at an early date. The date of Paul's meeting with him, Gal. 1:19, must have been about A.D. 36 or soon after. But this would be no more than a roundabout way of making Jude a brother of Jesus, in fact that very Judas mentioned in Mark 6:3. But the situation Jude attacks is certainly some seventy-five years after the writing of Galatians and more than a hundred years after the birth of Jesus' brothers.

Early Syrian writers make Judas son of James, Luke 6:16, identical with Thomas, rightly perceiving that Thomas is no name at all in Hebrew, but means twin, just as Didymus in Greek is not a proper name, but a Greek word meaning twin. But it is clearly Luke's intention to identify him with the Thaddeus who is tenth in the order of the Twelve in Mark and Matthew.

In both Luke's lists of apostles, Luke 6:16 and Acts 1:13, a "Judas, the son of James" is mentioned. He seems to take the place of Thaddeus of Matt. 10:3 and Mark 3:18. Is he the son of James the son of Zebedee, and was there then a father-son group within the Twelve? It is not impossible. But if so, what James is meant? James is simply our established English translation of Jacob, a name which occurs more than a hundred and fifty times in the Old Testament and the Apocrypha, mostly of course with reference to the son of Isaac, who was the progenitor of the Hebrew people. There were among the apostles James the brother of John, the son of Zebedee and Salome, and James the son of Alpheus. Did either have a son old enough to be one of the twelve apostles?

Jewish boys matured early. But would he not be mentioned then in connection with or at least in proximity to his father James? Perhaps not, if the order is at least in part one of apparent importance. And in point of proximity in Acts 1:13 this Judas is second from James son of Alpheus, as also in Luke 6:16. It is probably his name that is meant as that of the author of Jude.

Giving the little epistle his name would be like dedicating it to him today; it is thought of as being such a letter as he would have written, had he lived to witness the vagaries of Docetism.

First, Second, and Third John

The author of the Gospel of John wrote three letters, not at different times, but clearly at one time, for one is to a man named Gaius, another is to a church to which Gaius belonged, and one is to Christians in general to warn them against the Docetists, whose views and ways the Elder regarded as so dangerous to the Christian faith and life. It is plain that the Elder is sending his letter out to the churches of the Roman province of Asia, and with it he sends a short letter to the individual church, and a shorter one to a member of the church, so that the three are meant to go together. They will all be delivered to Gaius, who will then see that the church letter reaches that church, and it will then introduce the general letter, I John, to that church.

The long letter is a strong condemnation of the Docetic ideas that were threatening the churches early in the second century, and a noble statement of true Christian ideals in opposition to them. He introduces himself not at all in the Greek manner, with his name, followed by his father's name; no, he is simply "The Elder" and so it is to the Elder John, of Ephesus, that we must attribute the three letters and the

Gospel of John. For the letters and the Gospel are clearly by the same hand, and the same great ideas underlie them all, indeed it is in I John 4:8 that they reach their climax, their loftiest and profoundest statement—"for God is love!"

The Gospel and the letters are thoroughly Greek, in language, literary method, and basic interests and ways of expression. They show unmistakable acquaintance with Paul's published letters, which were collected and published soon after A.D. 90. The author is so well-known that he can identify himself simply as "The Elder"; he needs and claims no closer identification or higher title. These four writings afford no basis for thinking him the Apostle John, the brother of James, the fisherman of Galilee, and make no such claim. The Elder writes his letters to protect the churches from the errors of the rising sects, especially the Docetic sect, and to unite them against it; this is also the meaning of the intercessory prayer in John, chapter 17, which culminates in the petition that they all may be one, 17:20, 21.

10

THE APOSTOLIC FATHERS

A WHOLE VOLUME of writings of the late first and early second centuries have been assembled since 1672, as supposedly the works of the pupils and friends of the apostles, and further manuscript discoveries have somewhat enlarged their number. Modern research has considerably reduced their closeness to the apostolic circle, but their value for an approach to the beginnings of Christianity is second only to that of the New Testament itself. By 1699 they had come to be called the Apostolic Fathers, and they have since been republished and supplemented by further discoveries of manuscripts. Hardly one of their authors can be confidently said to have known the apostles, or any of them, and yet they importantly support and enrich our understanding of Christian beginnings.

The First Letter of Clement: To the Corinthians

The earliest Christian writing not in the New Testament that has come down to us from the first century is the Letter of Clement. It was written in the name of the church at Rome to the church at Corinth, very probably by that very

Clement who was bishop of Rome A.D. 88-97, in succession to
Linus and Anencletus. The church at Corinth was in a state
of insubordination against its presbyters or elders, and this
was becoming a scandal among the churches. The Roman
church had just been called upon by the Letter to the
Hebrews to take the lead in teaching the churches, Heb. 5:11
to 6:3: "For although from the length of your Christian
experience you ought to be teaching others, you actually
need someone to teach you over again the very elements of
Christian truth," 5:12.

It is this challenge which Clement or his spokesman seeks
to meet in this letter, which is somewhat longer than First
Corinthians, Paul's first letter to the same church; it almost
seems as though he intended not to fall short of it in length,
at any rate! It is a valuable example of early Christian preaching, for Clement really preaches to the Corinthians. His
allusions to or quotations from the Greek translation of the
Old Testament or the Christian writings already written
number over two hundred. His Christian library is already
noteworthy; he knows the Gospels of Matthew, Mark and
Luke, and the Acts; Paul's principal letters—Romans, I and II
Corinthians, Galatians, Philippians, Ephesians; his letter is
closely akin to I Peter, which was written from the Roman
church soon after. Of course he knows Hebrews, which had
virtually challenged the Roman church to take the lead in
advising and instructing the churches, Heb. 5:12. The Roman
church was making diligent use of the rising treasure of
Christian literature, which a few generations later formed the
New Testament.

First Clement has come down to us in the Codex Alexandrinus, a fifth-century manuscript of the Greek Bible, in
which it stands after the Revelation, and in an eleventh-
century manuscript discovered by Bryennius in 1873. There

are also versions of it in Syriac, Latin and Coptic. Paul mentions a fellow worker of his at Philippi, named Clement, Phil. 4:3, but we cannot surely identify him with the Clement who wrote this letter from Rome a generation later.

The Shepherd of Hermas

We have seen how the letter we call Hebrews, written to the Roman church about A.D. 95, stirred that church to take a much more active part in teaching and guiding the churches. It had moved Rome to write the letters we know as I Peter and I Clement, and now at the very end of the first century a prophet of the Roman church named Hermas was stirred by Hebrews to write the longest book Christians had yet produced, except the two-volume work of Luke, comprising his Gospel and the Acts. Hermas called his book *The Shepherd,* as he styled the angel of repentance. Hebrews taught with great sternness that there is no forgiveness for apostasy, 10:26-31: "It is a fearful thing to fall into the hands of the living God!" By apostasy, however, Hermas understands any sin after baptism, for which he declares there is no forgiveness, or rather there is forgiveness for falling into it once, but only once; after that never again!

He presents this in a series of conversations with the Shepherd, the angel of repentance whom Hermas questions, carefully recording his answers very much as in Second Esdras, a work contemporary with Hermas, Ezra puts his questions to the angel Uriel and writes down his answers. Yet we cannot suppose that Hermas knows II Esdras, a work written at the very same time with the Shepherd.

Hermas was a foundling and a slave; his first sentence reveals in a single line the hideous world into which he had been born: "The man who brought me up sold me to a woman named Rhoda in Rome." His book falls into three parts: five Visions or Revelations: twelve Commands and ten Parables, but some of these divisions are of inordinate length, so the book as a whole is fully three-fourths as long as Luke-Acts combined. It is an imaginative and highly varied narrative and enjoyed a great popularity in the Early Church. Yet very few manuscripts of it have survived.

Hermas' work began with a group of four Visions emphasizing repentance, and this was probably the first stage of his work; in his second Vision he says it is the duty of Clement to send copies of his book out among the churches, and this fixes the date of this first form of his book in the last years of Clement's episcopate, A.D. 95-97, to which also its dependence upon Hebrews points.

Then a few years later he wrote a longer book, *The Shepherd* properly so called, in which the figure of the Shepherd appears and is dominant. Hippolytus reports a statement that a new repentance was announced and preached in the Roman church in the third year of Trajan, which sounds like a reference to this work of Hermas demanding repentance, in A.D. 100.

Later still, these two books were combined, the *Visions* and *The Shepherd* making up the larger or complete *Shepherd*, which we know. It was accepted as a part of the New Testament by Clement of Alexandria, late in the second century, and by Origen in the first half of the third, and it found a place at the end of the great Sinaitic manuscript of the Bible, toward the middle of the fourth century. So highly was Hermas' book regarded in the Early Church. And in Dante's *Divine Comedy*, in 1300, Beatrice and Vergil, through whom he received his revelation, remind us of Rhoda and the Shepherd, through whom Hermas says he received his.

The Teaching of the Apostles

It was apparently the collection and publication of ten of Paul's letters with their great emphasis of faith as the indispensable and all-sufficient element in religious experience that spurred some rival spirit to write and publish the first form of what he chose to call *The Teaching of the Apostles,* or of the Twelve Apostles, seeking to emphasize what Peter and his associates had taught, in preference to Paul's doctrine of the adequacy of faith alone. While no complete text of this little tract has been found, and it was written about 100-110, long after the death of the last apostle, its influence may be traced in half a dozen later writers or writings: the *Didache,* or *Teaching;* the *Letter of Barnabas,* and the *Life of Schnudi.*

Paul's collected letters, ten in number, were published about A.D. 95, and made such an impression upon Christian thinkers and writers that while up to that time no Christian writer had shown any acquaintance with them or influence of them, after that every Christian writer did so! But the writer of the *Doctrina,* or *Teaching,* felt that Paul said too much about faith to the neglect of more tangible Christian attitudes, such as keeping the Ten Commandments, avoiding immorality, and in general living an upright life. He clearly felt that too much emphasis upon faith led to the neglect of the practical virtues, church attendance, benevolence and charity, and certainly Paul meant no neglect of them, as many passages in his letters such as I Corinthians, chapter 13, and Phil. 4:8, 9 are enough to show.

The opening lines of the *Doctrina,* as we may call it, for it has come down to us only in Latin, evidently translated from the Greek, will remind readers of the Dead Sea Scrolls, of the ways of Light and of Darkness there described. But it is always well to remember that God's first command in

Genesis is "Let there be light!" and God saw that the light was good!

Similar phraseology is found in the New Testament and the Apostolic Fathers. "You are all sons of light and sons of day," I Thess. 5:5; the sons of this age are contrasted with the sons of the light, Luke 16:8. "You must live like children of light," Eph. 5:8. " 'While you have the light believe in the light, that you may become sons of light,' " John 12:36. A generation later, after A.D. 150, the *Letter of Barnabas* speaks of the "Way of Light," 18:1; 19:1, 12. So that form of expression had been in Christian use from the oldest Christian letter, I Thessalonians, about A.D. 50, down. In John, Jesus declares, " 'I am the light of the world,' " see also 12:46, " 'I have come into the world as a light.' " Yet Matthew, written thirty years earlier, had said, " 'You are the light of the world!' " 5:14. We may compare the *War of the Sons of Light with the Sons of Darkness*, 1.

The Teaching of the Apostles was later, toward A.D. 150, enriched with texts from Matthew, Luke-Acts, I Peter, and the *Shepherd of Hermas*, to make up a little handbook on church rites and practices for rural and outlying congregations. Here was the Lord's Prayer, with other prayers, especially of thanksgiving. This tract from its Greek name is known as the *Didache* (Teaching).

There are also instructions in it on how to baptize and when to fast, for church and private use. This document, too, had a considerable influence among the churches and upon subsequent writers, especially upon such books as the *Didascalia*, late in the third century, and the *Apostolic Constitutions*, late in the fourth. It claimed the slightly more formal name of the *Teaching of the Twelve Apostles*.

Both these widely influential tracts were suggested and called forth by the extraordinary effect produced by the publication and continued spread of Paul's letters, over against which these two little writings claimed the authority of the twelve apostles. It plainly reflects the reasonable conviction of the Early Church that the twelve apostles of Jesus were authorized to organize the development and ways of worship of the churches that would be formed. But it cannot be shown that the apostles or any of them had anything to do directly with such matters, except as Peter so heroically preached and labored in Rome in the sixties, until it cost him his life. They must have been far more democratically worked out.

Indeed, it is at first sight from some points of view rather surprising that the apostolic band did not take it upon itself to do much more than it did in the directions of Christian liturgy and organization. But of course the explanation is right at hand. The primitive church believed profoundly in the early, almost the immediate, return of Jesus in Messianic judgment, see especially I Corinthians, chapter 15, and the closing verses of the Revelation. This was no atmosphere to call forth elaborate arrangements in organization or ritual.

In the second place, the Christian conviction that the spirit of Christ animated and guided his followers made any such preoccupation about organization and liturgy superfluous and even presumptuous. As Walter Pater said, in his *Marius the Epicurean,* in 1885, its liturgical genius was one of the spiritual endowments of the Early Church.

The Letters of Ignatius

Sometime early in the second century, between 107 and 117, Ignatius, the bishop of Antioch in Syria, was arrested and condemned to death. For some reason he was taken all the way to Rome for execution: he was to be thrown to the lions in the Coliseum. He must have been regarded as a prisoner of some consequence to have been taken so far just to be killed; it was probably his prestige as the head of the Christians in Antioch that caused it. Antioch was the chief Christian center of the eastern part of the Empire; indeed, it was called the queen of the East, and the third city in the Roman world ranking after Rome and Alexandria. It was also probably the most notoriously licentious and corrupt city in the empire. For such reasons, we may suppose, its bishop was to be taken all the way to Rome to suffer martyrdom.

As his guard of ten Roman soldiers—"leopards," he called them—took him through the province of Asia, as western Asia Minor was called, the churches moved by what was going on sought to welcome him and give him such Christian encouragement as they could. So it came about that the churches at Philadelphia and Smyrna, on his way, welcomed him, while those on the alternative route his guards might have followed, Tralles, Magnesia and Ephesus, sent delegations to greet him.

The principal bishops of the region, Onesimus of Ephesus and Polycarp of Smyrna, succeeded in reaching him with their encouragement, in helping him to send messages of gratitude to the churches which had so warmly welcomed him, as did an Ephesian deacon named Burrhus. As Ignatius seems to have written nothing before meeting the bishops at Smyrna and no more after leaving Burrhus at Troas, it seems probable that he wrote principally at their instigation. Evidently those three took charge of copying and delivering his letters. Ephesus was at that time the literary center of Christianity, and it was natural for them to encourage him to use his great prestige as a Christian confessor on his way to martyrdom, against Docetism, the most dangerous heresy of the day, and also to see to the immediate publication of the seven letters. Only a few years before, the bishops of these parts had collected and published the Letters of Paul, which had proved an amazing success, and other important Christian books had first found publication in the circle of Ephesus. Onesimus had brought Burrhus, who was evidently a competent scribe, from Ephesus to do the necessary writing for Ignatius, and Polycarp later circulated the letters, as his own letter to the Philippians, written right after Ignatius left Smyrna, shows. It was no accident that copies of the seven letters were kept together and survived through the centuries as a collection.

So it came about that Ignatius wrote from Smyrna letters to the churches of Ephesus, Magnesia and Tralles, acknowledging their sending delegations to greet him, and another to the church at Rome, urging them to make no efforts for his release. Then, when his guards hurried him on to Troas, he wrote from there letters to the Philadelphians, the Smyrnaeans and Polycarp, who had looked after him so assiduously.

From Troas he was taken to Neapolis and Philippi, where he disappears from us. Eusebius says he was martyred in A.D. 107-108, but modern learning places it about 110-117.

The letters reflect the mind of a deeply religious man facing a hideous and violent death, and at the same time warning the churches which had shown themselves his friends in his ordeal, against the errors and delusions of Docetism. The letters reflect the threefold ministry—bishops, elders or presbyters, and deacons. The longest of the letters, written to the Ephesians, is about the length of Paul's Letter to the Colossians. After the books of the New Testament that had been written, the letters of Ignatius are among the most primitive documents of Christianity. But it is clear that the alert men who enabled Ignatius to write them lost no time in giving them at least a limited publication among the churches immediately concerned.

The Ignatian letters have had a singular history. In Syriac they were reduced to three letters much abbreviated. But in

Greek and Latin they were individually enlarged by interpolation, or numerically increased by a string of spurious letters, or both, so that the Ignatian literature has had varied history.

The Letter of Polycarp to the Philippians

Polycarp's letter to the Philippians is a sequel to the Letters of Ignatius. Ignatius was brought by his guards from the coast of Asia to Philippi, in Macedonia, and seems to have told the Philippians who called upon him of the letters he had written while in Asia; he suggested that they should write Polycarp at Smyrna for copies of them. This confirms our impression that Polycarp and Onesimus intended to circulate the letters among the churches, to correct the teachings of the Docetic sect. Polycarp at once complied, not only sending the Philippians copies of the seven letters, but writing them a considerable letter of his own, which has come down to us as Polycarp *To the Philippians*. He says nothing about the threefold ministry, as Ignatius had done, but writes in the name of Polycarp and the elders who are with him, going on to discuss the duties of elders and of deacons at some length. No complete text of the letter has been found in Greek; the Greek manuscripts break off before the end of the ninth chapter, and Eusebius in his *Church History*, A.D. 326, obligingly supplies the thirteenth chapter. But the parts missing in the Greek, chapters 10-14, are supplied by a Latin version. It is about the length of Paul's Letter to the Philippians.

The Letter of Barnabas

While Barnabas was not one of the twelve apostles, he made a notable place for himself early in the Christian mission, and it was he who brought Paul out of his obscurity in Tarsus, Acts 9:26-30; 11:25. While Barnabas, a Jew of Cyprus, was no apostle, he soon made himself felt as an able missionary, and worked as long as we can trace his labors in the fullest co-operation with the leaders of the Twelve and with Paul, whom he really discovered and introduced to his career. His homeland of Cyprus became his particular missionary field, Acts 13:1-4; 15:39, after the First Missionary Journey.

Barnabas was a Levite. His real name was Joseph, but the apostles had named him Barnabas, which the Acts says meant "Son of Encouragement," Acts 4:36. No authentic writing of his has come down to us, but a "letter" bearing his name has long been extant in Latin, but was known only partially in Greek, until Tischendorf, in 1859, found it complete near the end of the Codex Sinaiticus, the great Greek Bible manuscript of the fourth century. When it was shown him at the convent on Mount Sinai on the last evening of his third visit, Tischendorf was so alive to its importance that he sat up all night to copy its Greek text, fearful that the manuscript might be taken from him next morning and never shown to scholars again! Fourteen years later, Bryennius found the letter in Greek at Constantinople in a manuscript dated A.D. 1056.

The presence of the "Letter of Barnabas" right after the book of Revelation, in the great Sinaitic manuscript, the oldest complete Greek manuscript of the New Testament known, shows how highly it was regarded in Egypt about A.D. 350. The great Alexandrian scholars Clement and Origen, late in the second century and in the first half of the third, accepted it as part of the New Testament, but in the years that followed it did not find general acceptance as such. For as the Stoics had allegorized Homer for their religious purposes, Barnabas seeks to allegorize the Old Testament, in fact, he believes that a wicked angel had deceived the Jews into taking it literally, not allegorically as Barnabas thinks they should have done. We call the letter by the name of Barnabas, though it was evidently written seventy-five years later than his time, probably not before the reign of Hadrian, and his erection of a temple of Jupiter in Jerusalem, in A.D. 130-131. A glimpse of the allegorical interpretation of Scripture meets us even in Paul, in Gal. 4:21-31. Yet one of Paul's leading traits is his aversion to such interpretation of the Old Testament! Allegory was so prevalent in his time that the allegorizers had made Homer the Bible of the Greeks, simply by treating its characters and incidents allegorically, instead of historically or realistically.

The Martyrdom of Polycarp

Few of the many martyrdoms that marked the rise of Christianity were recorded; we think of the Crucifixion, which was in the fullest and deepest sense a martyrdom; and of the stoning of Stephen, recorded in Acts 7:57 to 8:1. There was also the death of James, the third of the apostles, or in our earliest list, Mark 3:17, the second of them, so briefly reported in Acts 12:2; Herod Agrippa "had John's brother, James, beheaded." The death of Stephen, by stoning, is more particularly treated. But the first really full account of the seizure, trial, and execution of a Christian martyr is that of Polycarp, the venerable bishop of Smyrna, on February 22, A.D. 156.

Strangely enough, the fullest account of such cruel killings is given us by a Roman historian, Tacitus, in his *Annals*, 15:44, written probably between A.D. 110 and 120; we moderns can hardly bear to read it! Nero is trying to escape the blame for the burning of Rome in A.D. 64, by throwing it upon the Christians there. Tacitus says:

Hence, to suppress the rumor, he falsely charged with the guilt, and punished with the most exquisite tortures, the persons commonly called Christians, who were hated for their enormities. Christus, the founder of that name, was put to death as a criminal by Pontius Pilate, procurator of Judea, in the reign of Tiberius, but the pernicious superstition, repressed for a time, broke out again, not only through Judea, where the mischief originated, but through the city of Rome also, where all things horrible and disgraceful flow from all quarters, as to a common receptacle, and where they are encouraged. Accordingly, first those were seized who confessed they were Christians; next, on their information, a vast multitude were convicted, not so much on the charge of burning the city as of hating the human race. And in their deaths they were also made the subjects of sport, for they were covered with the hides of wild beasts, and worried to death by dogs, or nailed to crosses, or set fire to, and when day declined burned to serve for nocturnal lights. Nero offered his own gardens for that spectacle . . .

The date of these mass martyrdoms was August, A.D. 64. I cannot doubt that Heb. 10:32-34 refers to the same persecution, for Hebrews was clearly written to the church at Rome: "But you must remember those early days when after you had received the light you had to go through a great struggle with persecution, sometimes being actually exposed as a public spectacle to insults and violence, and sometimes showing yourselves ready to share the lot of those in that condition. For you showed sympathy with those who were in prison, and you put up with it cheerfully when your property was taken from you, for you knew that you had in yourselves a greater possession that was lasting."

One account of a Christian martyrdom has come down to us from the second century. It is that of Polycarp, bishop of Smyrna, who had so befriended Ignatius of Antioch when he was being taken to Rome for martyrdom, forty or forty-five years before. Irenaeus, the famous author of the *Refuta-*

tion of Gnosticism, A.D. 181-189, in his youth at Smyrna had seen Polycarp and heard him speak. Polycarp had himself written a letter to the Philippians and been active in circulating the Letters of Ignatius, indeed active in stimulating Ignatius to write them. Polycarp's martyrdom was recorded in some detail; the closing lines attribute it to a certain Irenaeus, "a disciple of Polycarp," but he can hardly be the Irenaeus of Lyons who about A.D. 180 wrote the famous *Refutation of Gnosticism,* though *he* had been a boy in Smyrna and could remember hearing Polycarp preach.

It is not without reason therefore that Polycarp with Onesimus have been styled Apostolic Fathers, since Onesimus in particular can be shown with some probability to have been none other than the slave boy of Philemon who was freed at Paul's request, Philemon 15-20, and then it would seem became a Christian leader of such stature that he was made bishop of Ephesus by 115 or 120, and co-operated with Polycarp in making it possible for Ignatius, although a prisoner, to meet Christian delegations and write a whole series of letters to churches. I have even felt that it was this very Onesimus who had long known of two letters of Paul, to the churches of Colossae and Laodicea, who, after Luke-Acts came out with the names of so many other churches which Paul had founded, thought of inquiring among them for any old letters of Paul's they might still possess, and so collected and published along with them the group of Paul's letters that from that time onward have so greatly influenced Christian thought! Certainly it was just then that Paul began to be felt in Christian writing, as he has never since ceased to be. When it is observed that Ephesians is unmistakably built upon the other nine, and in the oldest manuscripts mentions no church as particularly addressed, and reveals no specific church situation to be remedied, we may well suppose that what we call Ephesians was written to introduce the whole collection to Christians in general. It is certainly a striking fact that while up to that time no Christian writing (Mark, Matthew, Luke-Acts, Revelation) shows any literary influence of Paul's writings, after that time every Christian writing does so! And who would be more likely to concern himself to collect and publish them than the emancipated slave boy whom Paul had introduced to freedom and self-realization, Philemon 10? To no one could the letters to Colossae and Laodicea (Philemon) have meant anything like what they meant to him! And was he not just the man to put the means of writing a group of letters to churches into the hands of Ignatius, a prisoner for Christ's sake, just as Paul had been? The man's name is the same, and he has the same ways of working; what more proof do we want?

The Second Letter of Clement

What has come down to us as "Second Clement" is really a Christian sermon, written probably at Rome soon after the middle of the second century, by Soter, bishop of Rome, 166-174, sent to the church at Corinth as a letter and acknowledged by Dionysius, bishop of Corinth, in a letter fortunately preserved for us by Eusebius in his famous *Church History*, iv:23:11. Dionysius writes to Soter that the Corinthians will preserve his letter, and read it again and again, and be helped by it, as they are by "the former letter, written to us through Clement." It was evidently in this way that the second letter came to be preserved with the first, and both under the name of Clement, who had written the first one, seventy years before. It is no small gain to have another genuine Christian letter of such an early date.

Soter calls upon his hearers to repent of their sins and to serve God with all their hearts, and always to cling to their

Christian hope of resurrection. The writer shows that he has and uses the four Gospels and the Letters of Paul, and also First Peter and the Gospel of the Egyptians (A.D. 130-140). Besides these he has and quotes a strange prophetical work which Clement had quoted, which may be the lost book of Eldad and Modat, quoted by Clement in his letter and mentioned by Hermas in his book *The Shepherd*, written at the end of the first century, Visions ii. 3:4.

Second Clement, as Soter's letter came to be called, was preserved in the church chest at Rome along with First Clement, and the two were accepted as part of the New Testament in some Syriac and even Arabic copies, as well as in the Greek Codex Alexandrinus of the fifth century, in which First and Second Clement follow the Revelation of John.

Interpretations of Sayings of the Lord

Toward the middle of the second century there lived in Hierapolis, in Phrygia, only some fifty miles east of Ephesus, in the Lycus valley, a Christian named Papias. He had the interviewer's instinct, and when any elderly Christian passed that way, he made it his business to question such a man about any contacts he might have had with any of the apostles, and any memory he retained of what they had said. Hierapolis is once mentioned in the New Testament, in Col. 4:13, as already a rising Christian center, with the almost contiguous towns of Colossae and Laodicea; it was only six miles from Laodicea and twelve from Colossae, and Colossae and Laodicea were recipients of New Testament letters, Col. 1:2; Rev. 3:14. On a highroad of the Empire, it must have been often visited by travelers from east and west, many of them Christian believers.

Papias made it his business to call upon such strangers and

ask them for any such sayings or memories of the apostles as they might have. This earnest man proceeded to record these in a book for the benefit of his contemporaries and of posterity. This very modern idea (as we should consider it) resulted in a work in five books named *Interpretations of Sayings of the Lord*. It was known to Irenaeus, late in the second century, and used by Eusebius in his *Church History*. It was known to Jerome, who died in 420, to Philip of Side, about 430, to Andreas of Caesarea, late in the sixth century, to Maximus the Confessor, who died in 662, to Anastasius of Sinai, who died about 700, to Georgius Hamartolus, about 842, and to Photius, 890. The book was still being read in the ninth century, and old catalogs of the monastery libraries at Nismes, in southern France, and at Stams, in Austria, on the lower Inn, only twenty miles from Innsbruck, show that copies of it still existed there in 1218 and 1341. In fact Harnack spent a week at Stams hunting for it in the convent library, in vain! What a treasure it might prove is shown by the fragments that later writers preserved from it.

Eusebius preserves in his *Church History*, iii:39, some lines from Papias' own preface:

> "But I will not hesitate to put down along with my interpretations whatever I carefully learned at any time from the elders, and carefully remembered, assuring you of their truth. For I did not, like most people, enjoy those who have much to say, but those who taught what was true; nor those who relate commands of others, but those who report the ones given by the Lord to the faith and proceeding from the Truth itself. And if anyone should come my way who had been a follower of the elders, I would ask for the accounts given by the elders—what Andrew or what Peter said, or what Philip or what Thomas or James, or what John or Matthew said, or any other of the disciples of the Lord, and what Aristion and the elder John, the disciples of the Lord, say.

For I did not think that the contents of books would profit me
as much as what came from the living and surviving voice." . . .

And in his own writing he hands down other accounts, Eusebius goes on, given by Aristion, who has already been mentioned,
of the Lord's sayings, and traditions of John the Elder, to which
we refer the inquiring, but I must add to his utterances already
quoted a tradition about Mark who wrote the gospel, which he
sets forth in the following words:

"The Elder said this also: Mark had been the interpreter of
Peter, and wrote down accurately, though not in order, everything that he remembered that had been said or done by the
Lord. For he neither heard the Lord nor followed him, but afterward, as I said, attended Peter, who adapted his instructions to
the needs of his hearers, but had no design of giving a connected account of the Lord's oracles. So then Mark made no
mistake in thus writing some things as he remembered them, for
he made it his one concern not to omit anything that he had
heard, or to make any false statement in them."

This then is what Papias relates about Mark. But about Matthew he says this: "So Matthew composed the Sayings in the
Aramaic language, and everyone translated them as well as he
could."

The same man uses proofs from the First Epistle of John and
likewise from the epistle of Peter. And he relates another story
about a woman who was accused of many sins before the Lord,
which the Gospel according to the Hebrews contains. And this
also we must certainly take account of, in addition to what has
been stated.

This reference is clearly to the incident that in later manuscripts of John crept into its text at the beginning of chapter
8 as 7:53 to 8:11.

The strangest relic of Papias' book is his crude millennialism, which led Eusebius to describe him as of very limited understanding, but which rather attracted Irenaeus. It
appears in the following passage:

The days will come when vines will grow each with ten thousand shoots and ten thousand branches on each shoot, and ten thousand twigs on each branch, and ten thousand clusters on each twig, and ten thousand grapes in each cluster, and each grape when crushed will yield twenty five jars of wine. And when one of the saints takes hold of a cluster, another cluster will cry out, "I am better. Take me, bless the Lord through me." In the same way a grain of wheat will produce ten thousand heads, and every head will have ten thousand grains, and every grain will produce ten pounds of fine flour, bright and clean. And other fruits, seeds and grass will produce in corresponding proportions. And all the animals will use those foods that are the products of the soil and become in turn peaceable and in harmony with one another, and in complete subjection to man. . . .

But to believers these things are credible. And when Judas, the betrayer, refused to believe and asked, "How will such production be effected by the Lord?" the Lord said, "Those who reach those times will see."

These bold and rosy anticipations, certainly marked by Jesus' boundless imagination and sweeping rhetoric—what Chesterton called his gigantesque diction—have been generally set aside as the idle fancies of later millennialism. And yet as we look about us today, in a society certainly not Christianized but certainly not wholly free from Jesus' influence, we see resemblances to what is here forecast—vast surpluses and fabulous productions. When the plant breeder surveys his specimens, is it not as though one of them cried out, "I am a better specimen; take me"? Think of Burbank and Carver! But in other realms of human effort results are just as stupendous—travel and communication, by wire and without wire, radio, television, and now just opening before mankind the atomic age! No, Irenaeus was right in being attracted by the millennial picture ascribed to Jesus. Jesus saw the possibilities of the human mind as no other ancient did; why should we in the second half of the twentieth century underestimate his prescience? How moving that last line, in reply to Judas' doubt, "Those who reach those times will see." No, the world is not what it was in the days of Papias. Think of the modern harvester, and what it does toward feeding mankind, compared with the ancient sickle!

Not the least astonishing thing about Jesus was the way he thought. It is the amazing freedom with which his mind worked. It was not at all confined to the well-known Jewish grooves and ruts of his day. It would be vanity for us to say that he thought like a modern! What will they be saying a century or more after us? What was Jesus' word to Judas? "Those who reach those times will see!"

The Sermon on the Mount can be read aloud in twenty minutes. All that Jesus says in the Gospels can be read, and could conceivably have been uttered, in two hours. Think of it! In two hours—yes, in twenty minutes, to change the current of mankind! As one of his hearers said,

"'No man ever talked as he does!'"

11

THE EPISTLE OF THE APOSTLES

O NE of the most interesting of modern manuscript discoveries is that of the Epistle of the Apostles, published by Schmidt in 1919 from Coptic, Latin and Ethiopic sources, though no Greek form of it had yet been found. It appears that about the middle of the second century a Christian of Asia (the circle of Ephesus) gathered out of the Gospels, the Acts and other Christian writings what he thought of most worth and interest in the way of history, morals and hopes. He conceived it as a sort of summary of what was of most value in Christian thought and experience. It was a little more than half as long as the Gospel of Mark. Earlier in the century, men had written what they considered best in the *Teaching of the Apostles,* and a generation after our writer, somebody wrote what he called the Gospel of the Twelve Apostles! These are repeated efforts to revive, as their authors supposed, what the apostles, if they could be reached, would offer as the essence of the gospel message and story.

No mention of this work has turned up in any Christian writer, but sixty years ago a part of it was found in Coptic. A fragment in Latin came to light twelve years later, and about the same time the whole book was found in Ethiopic. It is interesting how these ancient tongues step forward almost responsively, one after another, with some contribution in the field of early Christian literature! On the basis of these sources the full text was published in 1919.

The anonymous writer's list of apostles, in whose names the book purports to be written, is John, Thomas, Peter, Andrew, James, Philip, Bartholomew, Matthew, Nathanael, Judas the Zealot, and Cephas—though John 1:42 explains that Cephas really means Peter, and Nathanael, John 1:45-51, is not listed in the Gospels or the Acts as one of the Twelve. The writer begins by warning his readers against false apostles, such as Simon Magus and Cerinthus, a sectarian teacher of about the end of the first century. The book begins with the Creation and the Incarnation, gives a list of Jesus' miracles and tells briefly of the Crucifixion, burial and Resurrection, followed by the reunion with the disciples in Galilee, when he tells them of his experiences in the other world. The apostles ask him when he will return, and he says when a hundred and fifty years have passed. He foretells the work and fate of Paul and commissions the apostles as "fathers, servants and masters." He interprets the parable of the bridesmaids; the wise ones were named Faith, Love, Grace, Peace and Hope, the foolish ones Knowledge, Understanding, Obedience, Patience and Compassion—names not unlike those of the girls in the *Shepherd of Hermas,* Parable 9:15, written about A.D. 100.

The writer shows knowledge of the four Gospels and the Acts, the Revelations of John and Peter, and probably of the letters of Ignatius and Barnabas, and the *Shepherd of Hermas;* possibly also of the Gospel of Thomas, so he has quite a Christian library. He finds the five loaves of Matt. 14:17 symbolic of our faith in the Father, the Redeemer, the Holy Spirit, the holy church, and the forgiveness of sins. This was just the period when the Roman church was first seeking to formulate its baptismal creed.

The writer fixes the Second Coming at the time "when a hundred and fifty years are past," and one is reminded that Justin Martyr, in his *Apology* describes Jesus as born a hundred and fifty years before he writes. But the writer of the letter may be counting from Jesus' Resurrection, not from his birth. While this little work did not leave much impression on Greek Christianity, it passed into at least three versions, Coptic, Latin and Ethiopic. It evidently sought to give believers a sort of summary of a Christian literature that in a little more than a hundred years was growing voluminous.

12

THE SECTARIAN GOSPELS

The Gospel of Peter

IT is a striking fact that after the publication of the four Gospels together, probably about A.D. 125, a whole flock of individual gospels sprang up, some claiming the authority of individual apostles, notably Peter, Thomas, Bartholomew, Andrew, Philip, and even Judas. One cannot resist the impression that one of the factors leading to this strange development was the statement ending the final conclusion, chapter 21, added to the Gospel of John when it was republished, along with the three earlier (Synoptic) Gospels. It is a conclusion not only of John but of the whole Fourfold Gospel collection, which was destined to have such prodigious consequences in after years. It ran:

"There are many other things that Jesus did, so many in fact that if they were all written out, I do not suppose that the world itself would hold the books that would have to be written."

This may well have seemed to some minds an invitation to supply some of this wealth of literature out of their own pious imaginations. Certainly we seek in vain among the so-called apocryphal gospels that followed for anything which can be considered genuine or historical. Some of the religious feeling in them is sound enough, if we may judge, but as in any sense historical fact or genuine sayings of Jesus we cannot accept them. They are only significant as illustrative of second-century religious experience and reflection. As such, however, it is of the keenest interest to serious students of the first impact of the combined Christian Gospels upon the Greek world of the second century.

For one thing, that impact had enormous literary consequences. It is easy to list thirty or forty Christian Greek writers who wrote and published useful and even valuable books on Christian life and experience in the second half of the second century—Justin, Melito and Hegesippus. Christian literature became an extensive field, for the preacher, the apologist and the historian. A whole Christian literature sprang into being in the wake of the published Letters of Paul and the Four Gospels.

Nor is it strange that some of the most important of these assumed the names of notable apostles as their writers. We may question the honesty of this procedure, but we must remember that these writers sincerely felt that they were possessed with the Holy Spirit and carrying on just what the apostles had begun. At any rate, in the second century at least three uncanonical gospels were well-known in Egypt— the Gospel according to the Egyptians, the Gospel according to the Hebrews and the Gospel of Peter. They were all written in Greek.

The Gospel according to the Egyptians seems to have been given that name because it was in use among the non-Jewish Christians in Egypt, in contradistinction to that "according to the Hebrews" which circulated among the Jewish Christians there. Only a few fragments of these once popular books have survived. Clement of Alexandria, early in the third century, mentions "Egyptians" and quotes a few words.

But half a century earlier, in II Clement, a letter from one church, probably Rome, to another, probably Corinth, part of a supposed conversation between Jesus and Salome is quoted, without disapproval.

In 1897 a papyrus was found at Oxyrhynchus in Upper Egypt, which contained a series of Sayings of Jesus (as they were entitled) which have some resemblance to the known fragments of the Gospel of the Egyptians. One of the most famous of these was

"Raise the stone, and there thou shalt find me;
Cleave the wood, and there am I"

on which Henry Van Dyke based a moving poem. This discovery stirred the religious world. What is probably a genuine portion of that gospel from the third century was discovered at the same site in 1903. It seems to have consisted of vigorous and often penetrating religious observations such as believers in Egypt possessed of the Mind of Christ considered themselves competent to make, in his name.

These second-century writings make no claim of apostolic authorship. And fairly considered, the closing words of John, chapter 21, so far from shutting the door upon further gospel writing, sounded to second-century readers much more like an invitation to it! As the foremost of the Twelve, Peter was the logical selection as such a gospel writer, regardless of the fact that as the chief voucher for the Gospel of Mark he already had practically one Gospel to his credit. Of the memories of Peter told in his sermons in Rome as the chief source of the Gospel of Mark, we have already spoken. Now, in total disregard of that fact, someone, probably in Syria, between A.D. 120 and 140 wrote in the first person singular and in Peter's name, this new gospel, to popularize the

Docetic view of Jesus—that Jesus was too divine to suffer what the older Gospels said he suffered and that his agonies were only apparent, not real.

Seventy years ago this was most of what was known of this little book, but in 1886 at Akhmim in Upper Egypt there was found a little parchment book which contained, along with a fragment of the so-called Revelation of Peter and thirty-two chapters of the Book of Enoch in a Greek translation, five leaves of the Gospel of Peter! It is clearly an embellishment, from the Docetic point of view, of the Crucifixion and Resurrection. So we may dismiss the Gospel of Peter as plainly an effort to push the Docetic theology back into the gospel story. It has really nothing to do with Peter at all, for in Mark nothing is clearer or more emphatic than the reality of Jesus' suffering, and Passion.

The Akhmim pages were evidently copied from a fragment, so that by the time they were copied, the Gospel of Peter was available only in scattered fragments; it had gone out of vogue; and as the handwriting of the fragment is clearly of the fourth century, we may suppose that this gospel had already disappeared from even such currency as it may have had in the third century. It was simply a heretical document written to support the weird views of the Docetic sect, which held that Christ only "seemed" to suffer (the Greek verb for "seem" is *dokeo*), and that physical indulgences are no concern of the spiritual life.

The Gospels of Thomas, Matthias, James, Judas and Philip

Thomas.—Origen once wrote (it was early in the third century): "The church has four gospels, the sects very many," and another such sectarian gospel is that bearing the name of Thomas. Origen, about 240, mentions it, as does his

Roman contemporary Hippolytus. The church historian Eusebius mentions it (A.D. 326) as does Cyril of Jerusalem in A.D. 348. Other writers connect it with different sects, some of which are little more than names today, Irenaeus (apparently) with the Marcosians, Hippolytus with the Naasenes, or serpent worshipers, and Cyril with the Manichaeans! Into the vagaries of these forgotten sects we need hardly go. They are quite enough to show that the Gospel of Thomas had little to do with the historical origins of Christianity; it was a wildly fanciful creation, telling the story of Jesus' childhood from the Gnostic point of view.

Matthias.—Another such schismatic gospel was written in the second century, probably in Egypt, in the name of that Matthias who was appointed by the apostles to take the place of Judas, Acts 1:23-26. There was nothing particularly heretical about it, for Clement of Alexandria quotes it with apparent approval. It seems to have consisted of philosophical reflections upon Christian belief, with no fresh historical information upon the gospel story.

None of these gospels had any historical connection with the twelve apostles or any of them. The names given them were simply to attract readers to their contents. And they lead us to the paradoxical conclusion that the Gospel which really embodies Peter's memories and attitudes goes by the name of Mark, who shaped it; while Peter's name was later given to a far less faithful and significant story.

James.—Perhaps the most surprising of these second-century books claiming apostolic vouchers is the Book of James, also called the Gospel of James the Less—meaning Jesus' brother, who played such a leading part in the early development of the Jerusalem church after the Crucifixion and Resurrection, Gal. 1:19. It supports the Virgin Birth of Jesus and the perpetual virginity of Mary, in great detail. It begins with an account of the conception and birth of Mary herself, her presentation in the Temple at the age of three, and how she was kept there through her childhood until at the age of twelve she is married to Joseph, a widower with a number of sons. The Annunciation, conception, journey to Bethlehem and birth of Jesus in a cave there are then related. At the moment of Jesus' birth all nature stops transfixed. The astrologers bring their gifts, Herod kills the infant children, hoping to kill Jesus among them; John is preserved, but Herod puts Zechariah to death. In conclusion, "James" (the Lord's brother) declares himself the author and states that the book was written in Jerusalem.

While the book has suffered some accretions and alterations, the main narrative was doubtless written about A.D. 200. Of course, the whole picture of Mary's life from her infancy to the age of twelve in the Temple at Jerusalem is as totally and absurdly unhistorical as anything that could be imagined. Judaism was a man's religion, and the Temple was the last place where a tiny girl of three would be sent to be brought up. Nothing could have been more totally repugnant to Judaism. Yet the Book of James, or the Protevangelium survived and was widely popular, even entering into the Golden Legend, in 1275, and being brilliantly reflected in the works of the Italian painters—Giotto, Raphael, Titian, Ghirlandaio, and others. The Jews had no marriage ceremony; the man simply took the bride from her father's house to his house, that was all, unless he gave a dinner for his men friends, but of course the bride did not appear at that; that would have been the height of indelicacy. A wedding in the Temple is, under Judaism, simply unthinkable. The story is much influenced by the account of the birth of Samuel in First Samuel, chapter 1. The Decree of Gelasius (sixth century) repudiated the little book as heretical.

Judas.—To write a gospel in the name of Judas, the betrayer of Jesus, would seem so absurd as to be positively indecent, and yet the sectarian imagination of the second century was equal to it. Irenaeus tells of it (A.D. 181-189). He says it was the work of a sect appropriately known as the Cainites, belonging to the Valentinian wing of Gnosticism, and put forward the idea that Judas had a deeper knowledge of the truth than the eleven disciples, and this led him to betray Jesus. Epiphanius, writing about A.D. 376, also mentions it.

Philip.—Probably colored by Gnostic speculations was the Gospel of Philip, written perhaps by the end of the second century, simply as a vehicle for the speculations of the Gnostics, who believed that through revelation they had become possessed of a peculiar mystical "Knowledge" (Gnosis), such as the names of the demons, etc., which would enable the soul to subdue them on its heavenward way.

A Gospel of Bartholomew is also mentioned by Jerome, in a list of uncanonical gospels, but we are not sure that such a book existed. It may have been his way of alluding to Bartholomew's mission to "India," really meaning the region of the Bosporus, then included in India in the broad sense.

It is clear that the writers of these schismatic and heretical gospels, in seeking ancient authors to whom to assign their gospel efforts, liked best to use those of such apostles as seemed most likely to win a hearing for their eccentric writings.

13

THE ACTS OF THE INDIVIDUAL APOSTLES

Paul, John, Peter, Thomas and Andrew

The Acts of Paul[1]

SOON after the middle of the second century the imaginative movement that had created a whole series of apocryphal gospels, perhaps under the suggestion of the last verse in John, went on to the apostles and sought to build them up to satisfy Christian curiosity, and also to some extent to aid Christian devotion. The Acts leaves Paul's fate obscure; these Christian novelists—if we may so describe them; the Greeks had just invented the novel—undertook to fill in the gaps in his story and then passed to the other apostles and what became of them. The result was the Acta literature of the second and third centuries, written partly to edify and instruct but chiefly to entertain Christian readers.

Serious Christian historians paid little attention to this literature. Jerome late in the fourth century speaks of the fable of the baptized lion, and rejects it *in toto*. Commodian,

---

[1] Though Paul was not one of the Twelve, his Acts are included here because they formed with those of the other four, a recognized fivefold collection of such Acts.

the fifth-century Christian poet, speaks of a talking lion, which reminds us of the Roman story of Androcles and the Lion, revived from antiquity a generation ago with such success by George Bernard Shaw, in his play. Hippolytus of Rome, early in the third century, speaks with apparent approval of the story of a lion let loose upon Paul to devour him, which fell down and licked his feet instead! All this was in a measure cleared up when I found, in an Ethiopic manuscript in London, just such a story of Paul and a talking lion which Paul converted and baptized—evidently a stray chapter from the Acts of Paul. The Ethiopic went on to tell how later in the amphitheater a lion was let loose upon Paul to devour him, but curled up at his feet like a lamb instead. Then in 1936 Carl Schmidt and my old friend Wilhelm Schubart, with whom I shared the Greek papyrus workroom in the Berlin Museum in my student days, published from Greek manuscripts the bulk of these long-mysterious Acts of Paul, containing with much besides the whole story of Paul's converted and baptized lion, very much as I had found it in Ethiopic thirty years before. This completely accounted for the references in Hippolytus, Jerome and Commodian which had so long been so obscure.

In this gradual way the strange fairy-story literature about the apostles and their individual "Acts" sprang up in the latter half of the second century and the first half of the third. It contributes almost nothing to our knowledge of their actual work and fates, only revealing the keen interest in anything that could be said about them in the life of the expanding church. This was just one minor strain in the varied and growing literature of Greek Christianity in that age of persecutions. We in an age so given to fiction as our own can hardly blame the Christian writers who appropriated some of the techniques of the Greek novel, which was invented in the first century, to the use of the new faith. We may perhaps not unfairly compare it with a recent era of Sunday-school book literature, little of which aimed at being historical or factual. And as for its talking lions, that was the mood of Aesop and was not supposed to deceive anybody. Yet the official church, when asked to express its judgment, disapproved, and the author of the Acts of Paul when he acknowledged its authorship was not permitted to remain an elder in the church.

Yet the mood of the church in general was not in accord with church authority in this matter, and this fanciful interest in the fate of Paul in particular led to an imaginative effort to prolong the narrative of his career, which the Acts of the Apostles left so incomplete and uncertain. Of course Luke was not writing a biography of Paul, but the story of the rapid spread of Christianity over the Roman world. When Paul made contact with the church at Rome, the capital of the Empire, the story was told!

While the manuscript found by Schmidt and Schubart in Hamburg in 1927 gives us only the conclusion of these Acts, yet combined with the scattered episodes in other sources they give us the following story, which was cherished by Christians of the third and fourth centuries, at any rate as literature if not as history. We observe that, while the story of Paul in the Acts of the Apostles has little of the miraculous, these later Acts of Paul abound in it.

So if we piece together what these fragmentary manuscripts, Coptic, Greek, Ethiopic, etc., provide, we find perhaps a dozen episodes in Paul's adventurous travels.

1. Paul is at Pisidian Antioch, as in Acts 13:14. There he restores a dead Jewish boy to life. The boy's parents are converted, but the townspeople become incensed with the missionaries and drive Paul from the town.

2. As in the Acts, 13:51, he proceeds to Iconium. And now follows the episode so popular with the ancients that it was

for generations the only story in the book to survive, and lived on as The Acts of Paul and Thecla. The opening sentence has always seemed very abrupt, but of course it was simply the transition to the new scene. Thecla, a young lady of Iconium, is converted and breaks her engagement to marry, and although thrown to the wild beasts in the amphitheater, escapes and becomes a teacher of her new faith. This story reveals the book's chief interests—aversion to marriage and willingness to have women teach the new faith, in contrast with I Tim. 2:12.

3. At Myra, Paul cures a man of dropsy, thus deeply offending the man's son, who was hoping soon to inherit his father's property! The son is struck blind, but repents and is cured.

4. Paul leaves Asia Minor by way of Perga and visits Sidon, where the people shut him and his friends up in the temple of Apollo, but a part of it collapses in the middle of the night, which further incenses the Sidonians. They hurry Paul and his companions to the theater, with dire intentions, but what happened there is missing.

5. Paul next appears at Tyre, heals the sick, and preaches about Judaism.

6. He is next heard of at some mines, no one knows where, but a woman named Frontina, who has been converted, is thrown from a cliff and killed. Paul restores her to life, however, and takes her home through the town; the townspeople are at once won to the new faith.

7. Here the Greek manuscript places a story told by Nicephorus, about 1320, of a visit to Ephesus, not mentioned in the Coptic fragments but now supplied in detail by the new-found Greek text, which begins with this Ephesian episode: At Ephesus Paul is thrown into prison. In the prison he is visited by two women who are believers and wish to be baptized. Paul escapes from the prison long enough to

baptize them on the seashore. He is recaptured or returns
to his prison, and the next day is thrown to a huge lion in
the stadium. But the lion quietly curls up at his feet like a
lamb. (Hippolytus refers to such an incident.) The lion
speaks to Paul, and Paul asks him if he is not the lion Paul
had previously met and baptized. The lion replies that he is.
This story of the baptized lion—Jerome's "fable of the baptized lion" which he not unnaturally rejected—is told in detail in the Ethiopic Epistle of Pelagia, which tells of Paul's
first encounter with the lion, while on a journey, when Paul
baptized him, and goes on to relate Paul's later encounter
with the lion in the stadium, just as the newly discovered
Greek portions of the Acts of Paul now describe it! This
short martyrdom, which I had the good fortune to unearth
in an Ethiopic manuscript in the British Museum many years
ago, offered the first explanation of the baptized lion mentioned by Jerome, and the talking lion spoken of by Commodian, which had previously been so perplexing. Harnack
pooh-poohed this suggestion, but it was welcomed by Krü-
ger, and the Greek manuscript discovered by Schmidt and
Schubart definitely establishes its place as a part of the Acts
of Paul.

The Greek story continues with a great hailstorm, which
comes on and kills many of the spectators and the animals,
and cuts off the governor's ear! He is converted. The lion
escapes. Paul is released and proceeds to Macedonia.

8. The next division of the narrative is headed in the Greek
"From Philippi to Corinth," but nothing is said of the stay
in Philippi. The Coptic, however, relates that while in
prison there Paul received a short letter from the Corinthians, telling of the appearance among them of two false
teachers, Simon and Cleobius, and Paul writes a letter to the
Corinthians in reply. (This is the letter anciently accepted

by Syrian and Armenian churches as III Corinthians.) As
Paul takes leave of the Philippians, a local prophet and
prophetess there predict his work and fate in Rome.

9. The Greek account proceeds with the story of Paul's
stay in Corinth. The brothers there are grieved with his
conviction that he must go on to Rome. He embarks on a
ship, the captain of which had been baptized by Peter!

10. On the voyage Jesus appears to Paul, walking on the
water, and urges him on to Rome. He goes before the ship,
guiding it on its way like a star. As Paul lands, Jesus appears
again, and says, "I am going to be crucified again." (This is
an evident echo of the famous saying to Peter.) Paul is welcomed by the brethren at Rome, and addresses them. He is
tried, apparently before Nero, and executed with the sword,
but later reappears to Nero and his attendants and declares
that much evil will overtake him, in no long time, for the
righteous blood he has shed. Here the title, "Acts of Paul,"
in the Greek manuscript, marks the end of the book.

This is perhaps two-thirds or three-fourths of the whole
Acts of Paul. Jerome says, "The travels of Paul and Thecla
and the whole fable of the baptized lion, we reckon among
the apocryphal writings." Commodian says of God's power,
"For Paul, when he preached, he made a lion speak to the
people with a God-given voice." In the Ethiopic Epistle of
Pelagia, another of Paul's reputed converts, Paul meets a
huge lion on a mountain. They become friends and the lion
asks to be baptized. Paul complies. Later, when a woman
named Pelagia is converted and leaves her husband, Paul is
arrested, and a huge lion is loosed upon him in the "Theater." But it is the baptized lion, and he and Paul pray and
converse. They let Paul go "with his lion," but Pelagia suffers martyrdom. It is now clear that the lion episodes are from
the Acts of Paul; here are Jerome's baptized lion and Com-

modian's talking lion; they are one. The story of Pelagia also
exhibits the same aversion to marriage that we find in the
story of Thecla.

The Acts of John

The earliest of these Apocryphal Acts are those of John,
written probably by the middle of the second century, by a
certain Leucius, said to have been a disciple of John. It is
said to have been about the length of the Gospel of Matthew,
when complete, though now the beginning of the book and
some further episodes are lost. It seems to have dealt with
the arrest of John and his banishment to Patmos, the rugged
island in the Aegean not far from Ephesus. This at once
warns us that the writer identifies John the Prophet of
Ephesus, who wrote the Book of Revelation, Rev. 1:4, with
the Apostle John.

The first extended portion finds John visiting Ephesus,
where a man named Lycomedes is grieving over the illness
of his wife Cleopatra. He begs John to help him, and even
dies of grief. Cleopatra dies also, but John restores them both
to life. Lycomedes in gratitude has a painter come and paint
John's portrait. When John sees the portrait, he calls upon
Lycomedes to paint his own portrait, using as his colors
faith, knowledge, godly fear, meekness, kindness, and a
whole series of Christian virtues, and present it to Jesus
Christ.

The second narrative begins with the coming of brethren
from Miletus to John, to get him to go with them to Smyrna,
further up the coast, but he puts on black, and conducts
them to the temple of Artemis, the chief seat of idolatry in
Ephesus, where he mounts a high pedestal and challenges
the power of the goddess. Half the temple immediately falls
in ruins, and the idolaters then destroy the remaining half.

(As a matter of historical fact, the temple of Artemis was destroyed by the Goths in A.D. 262.) The Ephesians then turn to God and gather about John, who even raises from the dead the deceased priest of Artemis, who seems to have died in the destruction of her temple.

John next raises to life an old man just murdered by his profligate son, whom John then converts to the Christian life. This is followed in some texts by the story of John and the Partridge which may have belonged to the Acts. John was watching a partridge playing in the dust, and even stroking it and petting it, when a hunter (some accounts say a priest) came by and was offended by such frivolity on the part of such an august person. John inquired of the hunter whether he always kept his bow strung, and he said "No," because that would spoil its strength. John said the human mind is like that. The story resembles one in Aesop, of most uncertain date.

John visits Smyrna and Laodicea, names reminiscent of the seven churches of the Revelation, 1:11, and returns to Ephesus. On the way, stopping with his companions at a deserted inn, he finds it infested with bedbugs, but when he commands them to go away and not molest the servants of God, his companions laugh, but the bedbugs obey. John is struck with the fact that these poor creatures obey the voice of a man, but human beings disregard even that of God.

John is enthusiastically welcomed by the brethren at Ephesus, where he lodges at the house of Andronicus. This man's wife, Drusiana, wished to remain virgin, whereupon he had shut her up in a tomb to die. She does die, but after a series of horrible adventures John raises her from the dead and tells them a strange story of the various forms in which Jesus had been known to himself and his brother James when they were his first disciples in Galilee—now as a child, now as a youth, and now as middle-aged. He said that Jesus

in those Galilean days had been sometimes material, sometimes immaterial. A grotesque story follows, of the Twelve
before the arrest forming a circle with Jesus in the center,
the Twelve crying "Amen" to each of his mystic declarations,
beginning
"I would be saved, and I would save."
The mystic numbers twelve and eight (the Ogdoad) are
especially emphasized. The quaint practices of the mystery
cults of the time are clearly reflected in this symbolic dance
and its paradoxical responses. This mystic dance with its
chanted responses, so repugnant to the spirit of historical
Christianity, no doubt reflects the Gnostic rites and formu-
las of the second century.

At the hour of the Crucifixion John finds himself in a cave
and has the vision of the Cross of Light, with such a revelation of Christ himself and his Passion that John saw how
unreal all earthly persecutions were in comparison.

After further edifying wonders at Ephesus, with Atticus,
Eugenius, and Aristodemus the high priest of the local idolatry, John asks his disciples to dig a grave for him, then lies
down in it and peacefully expires.

The Acts of Peter

The Acts of Peter is preserved only in fragments, the first
in Coptic, the second principal part in Latin, and the Martyrdom of Peter in five oriental languages, and the Slavonic.
It was written probably in Asia Minor, toward the end of
the second century.

The Coptic fragment tells the extraordinary story of Peter's
daughter, who when little more than a child is seen by a
very rich man named Ptolemaeus who is so much in love
with her that when Peter refuses to let him have her he
simply comes and carries her off. Peter prays to God to

protect her, and she is stricken with paralysis. Then Ptolemaeus' servants bring her back to Peter's house.

Her sad condition perplexes people bringing their sick to Peter to be healed; why does he neglect his own daughter? Peter called his daughter to him and she rose and walked to him. At his command she then returns to her couch and her paralyzed condition. Peter considered this better than a life of shame. Ptolemaeus goes blind, repents, and dies, leaving Peter's daughter a valuable piece of property, which Peter devotes to charity.

A somewhat similar story about Peter is that of the gardener's daughter. A gardener asked Peter to pray for his virgin daughter, his only child. Peter did so, and she immediately fell dead. The old gardener besought Peter to raise her up again, and Peter did so. But soon after she was ravished by a slave, who ran away with her, and they both disappeared. This was probably the foil for the story of Peter's daughter. Peter is said to have told people who had lost their daughters, to think how many disasters of the world they had escaped.

The longest part of the Acts of Peter that has been preserved is in a Latin manuscript of the seventh century at Vercelli. It relates that Peter is released from his imprisonment in Rome and goes to Spain, leaving the church at Rome without a leader. This gives our old friend Simon Magus (the magician, of Acts 8:9-24) a chance to visit Rome, and the church, left without a head, sinks to seven members. Peter reaches Jerusalem, where a vision warns him that his old enemy of Samaria is creating trouble in Rome. Moreover, the twelve years Jesus had, in the so-called *Preaching of Peter*, told the apostles to stay in Jerusalem were now over, so Peter felt at liberty to return to Rome. But the ship is becalmed, and the crew gets drunk; in this dire situation the captain is converted; Peter even slides down a rope to baptize him in the sea! Reaching Italy, they land at Puteoli, as Paul had done, Acts 28:13, and make their way to Rome, where Peter encourages the believers, and even knocks at Simon's door, but the porter tells him Simon is not in. Peter then gives the watchdog his message, and the dog is immediately endowed with speech and goes in and delivers it. Peter sees a dried herring in a shop, puts it in water, and brings it back to life. He enables a baby only seven months old to talk. Peter tells the Roman Christians how back in Palestine a woman had been robbed by Simon and his crew, but the crime was revealed to him in a vision, and he had recovered and restored what she had lost.

A woman of ill repute brought Peter a large gift of money. People protested that he should not accept it, because of her bad character. They considered it tainted money. Peter only laughed and told them the money was really just a debt she owed to Christ.

A senator named Marcellus had entertained Simon in his house. Peter shows him his error in doing this, and he sprinkles his house with holy water to purify it, and then presents it to the church for a church or convent. The old women and widows are to come and pray in it, and each should receive a piece of gold for doing so. Peter visits the house, hears the gospel read in the dining hall and preaches in it. He tells the story of the Transfiguration with such power that his listeners see Christ in a vision; to some he appears as old, to others as young, to some even as a child—chapter 21; a rather Docetic picture drawn from the Acts of John, chapter 87. Stages are put up in the Forum and multitudes of people pay a piece of gold each to witness the contest that is to be arranged between Peter and Simon. The prefect calls upon Simon to show his power by killing one of his pages, and Simon complies. Peter is then called upon to bring the boy back to life, and he does so.

From this point on the Acta are extant in Greek as well as Latin manuscripts. Simon Magus, who has been amazing the people of Rome by flying over the city, declares that he will do so again, but Peter prays earnestly that he may fall and break his leg in three places, and he does. He loses his standing with the populace, leaves Rome and dies at Terracina.

Peter has been urging wives to leave their (pagan?) husbands, and this incenses the leading Romans against him. He is warned of his danger and starts to leave the city for a place of safety, but as he is getting out of Rome he meets Jesus himself, entering it! He asks him,

"Lord! Where are you going?" (*Domine, quo vadis?*)

Jesus answers that he is going into the city to be crucified again. Peter recognizes the rebuke, and turns back into the city, where he is crucified, but at his own request head downward.

The noble story of Peter's martyrdom does much to make up for the trivial and even heathen elements in so much of these Acts, written a full century and a half after the events with which they deal. Origen says that the Acts of Paul contained Jesus words, "I am going to be crucified again," and the newly discovered Acts of Paul contain the words. So evidently the writer of the Acts of Peter had the Acts of Paul before him. Peter's parting words to his wife as she was being led out to martyrdom are recorded by Clement of Alexandria in his *Miscellanies* and repeated by Eusebius in his *Church History:* "They say that when the blessed Peter saw his own wife led out to die, he rejoiced because of her summons and her return home, and called to her very encouragingly and comfortingly, addressing her by name, and saying,

" 'O thou, remember the Lord!' "

The Acts of Thomas

It was early in the third century that some Syrian Christian, probably at Edessa in Syria, wrote the Acts of Thomas. The book is in thirteen acts, culminating in the martyrdom of Thomas. Christianity had entered eastern Syria with Tatian, who had interwoven the four Gospels into his *Diatessaron*, and introduced the gospel in that form in Syriac about A.D. 172. In the same period Bardaisan, A.D. 154-222, had cultivated Christian literature among the Syrians with his poems. We do not know what hand if any he may have had in the Acts of Thomas, but it shows clear traces of Syriac poetry and liturgy. Whether the work as a whole was written in Syriac, or in Greek, as Montague James thought, is uncertain. It is the longest of the five books of individual apostolic Acts, and exists in Syriac and Greek, as well as in Armenian, Ethiopic and Latin versions.

It is a very ascetic document, telling of the efforts of Thomas to abolish the marriage relation and to get wives to leave their husbands. This seems strangely forgetful of Jesus' own words in Matt. 19:6 and Mark 10:9: "What God has joined together, man must not try to separate." It relates the introduction of the gospel into India, and indeed there is reason to think Christianity reached the shores of India soon after the beginning of the third century, if not in the first, as Syrian Christians there hold; some of the names mentioned in the Acts of Thomas are known to history, such as King Gundafor (Hyndopheres), who was king of part of India in the first century after Christ. But we cannot claim any historical value for these Acts of Thomas, which are full of suggestions of Gnostic, Mandaean and Manichaean religion. The ancient religious vocabulary of demon and wonder pervades them. The dead are raised, devils are cast out, and cures are worked by relics.

The book abounds in long speeches, prayers and hymns, and yet its thirteen acts are full of vigorous action:

1. The first act begins with a piece of humor that is fairly shocking. When the apostles draw lots for their mission fields Thomas draws India, which he declines. Jesus, however, without his knowledge sells him as a slave to an Indian merchant who is in search of a carpenter for the Indian king Gundafor, who is known to have reigned over a part of that country in the first century. The merchant accordingly claims Thomas as his slave and takes him off to India. Arrived at Andrapolis, Thomas finds the king's daughter is just about to be married. At the marriage Thomas utters a mystic bridal song and persuades the bride and groom to renounce marriage, chapters 1-16.

2. The same humorous quality appears in the second act, the heavenly palace. The king sets Thomas to build a palace for him, giving him the necessary money. Thomas gives it to the poor and when the king wishes to see what progress is being made, tells him that the palace is in heaven. The king is angered by this, but his brother dies and sees the palace in heaven. Miraculously restored to life, he tells the king about it.

3. A serpent has killed a woman's lover. Thomas forces the serpent to confess the act and all his other crimes; he brings the youth back to life, kills the serpent and converts the youth. The whole city repents.

4. A colt invokes blessings upon the apostle, and Thomas responds with a hymn of praise to Christ, which rather resembles the Isis litany found at Oxyrhynchus. He then talks with the colt and dismisses it. The colt falls dead.

5. A woman who has been troubled with a devil of lust implores the aid of Thomas. He casts out the devil, and it departs in fire and smoke. Then Thomas prays to Christ, and

baptizes the woman and her friends. When Thomas gives them the Communion, he marks the bread with a cross.

6. A young man who has murdered his mistress confesses his sin to Thomas. The apostle brings her back to life, and she tells them about the punishments of the lost, chapters 55-57, in language evidently drawn from the second-century *Revelation of Peter*. Thomas calls upon the people to repent, and they do so.

7. A captain beseeches Thomas to come and cure his wife and daughter, who are troubled by devils, and Thomas accompanies him.

8. On their way, the mules or horses drawing their car give out, and Thomas calls upon four wild asses to take their places. Arriving at the house, Thomas sends in one of the asses to call the demons out. The women come out, and with the aid of the wild ass Thomas effects their cure. The apostle then sends the four wild asses back to their pasture ground.

9. A woman named Mygdonia is converted and leaves her husband Charis. He has Thomas thrown into prison. In the prison Thomas utters the Hymn of the Soul, or of Redemption, the finest and most perplexing of such liturgical pieces in the Acts of Thomas. It tells how a prince goes down to Egypt to recover a pearl, but in Egypt forgets his errand, until a letter from home rouses him to obtain it, resume his royal attire and return home.

10. Thomas leaves the prison long enough to baptize Mygdonia. The king Misdai releases him, commanding him to reconcile Mygdonia to her husband.

11. But now Misdai's wife Tertia is converted and decides to leave him.

12. The king's son Vazan joins the disciples of Thomas, and follows him back to prison, where the apostle preaches and prays.

13. Thomas' principal converts join him in the prison; they

all go to Vazan's house; Vazan and the others are baptized and given Communion.

The thirteen acts are followed by the Martyrdom of Thomas, for Misdai condemns him to death, and he is taken up into a mountain and killed with spears. But later Misdai himself is converted.

Yet the Acts of Thomas is not without its humorous aspects, as when the Indian king is informed of Thomas' ascetic practices—that he fasted and prayed continually, ate nothing but bread with salt, drank nothing but water, and wore only one garment, the same one, summer and winter alike, and the Acts says, "The king rubbed his face with his hands, and shook his head for a long time"! It was too much for him.

The Acts of Andrew

The movement toward Christian fiction in the second and third centuries did not neglect the very obvious figure of Peter's brother Andrew, the second man called to be a follower, and later an apostle of Jesus, Mark 1:16, 18; 3:17. It was about the middle of the third century, perhaps as late as A.D. 260, that a Christian writer, in Greece or Asia Minor, wrote an imaginative account of the travels and wonders and teachings of Andrew. The story is made the vehicle of the current teaching that converted women should leave their heathen husbands and that marriage in general should be discouraged. It was probably felt that a higher level of sanctity would be thus attained.

This work has for the most part disappeared. The chief episode to survive is the story of the wife of the proconsul of Greece, a woman named Maximilla, and her efforts to separate from her husband, whose name was Aegeas, or Aegeates. Andrew urges her on in this course; his success leads Aegeates to arrest him and have him crucified at Patrae (the modern Patras) in Greece. Andrew lingered for three days on the cross, to which he was evidently bound, in the usual manner (not nailed).

The Acts declares that he preached most of this time to the crowds of believers who surrounded his cross. The Acts says nothing about the shape of his cross being unusual, but later tradition declared it was not T-shaped but X-shaped (the *crux decussata*) and this came to be known as St. Andrew's cross—the shape of the Greek letter Chi.

The preservation of what we have of the Acts of Andrew we owe to Gregory of Tours (538-594), who found a copy of the book in Greek and made a Latin abbreviation of it, leaving out most of the long discourses, we may suppose, and making the most of Andrew's miracles. While Eusebius, in A.D. 326, had said that Andrew's mission field was Scythia, north of the Black Sea, the Acts locates it in western Asia Minor, Macedonia and Greece, where Andrew finally suffers martyrdom, at Patrae, still a well-known port at the mouth of the Gulf of Corinth.

The impulse to Christian fiction that had found such varied expression in the five books of personal apostolic Acts in the second and third centuries found a fresh expression in the beginning of the fourth century, probably 313-325, in the *Recognitions* and the *Homilies* of Clement. The *Recognitions* purports to be written in the first person by Clement of Rome, its third bishop, A.D. 88-97, telling of his journey to Palestine, where he met Peter. He stays with Peter, and they discuss all sorts of matters of religion and doctrine. The excitement is provided by Clement's most providential finding and "recognition" of his long-lost parents and brothers, from whom he had been separated since his childhood. He is represented as writing this long account of it for James the brother of Jesus, who came so soon into the leadership of the Jerusalem church, Gal. 1:19; 2:9. There is something almost modern about the quaint representation of Clement, in a sort of quiet search for his lost relatives, which gives a spice of personal interest to what might otherwise appear very speculative and remote discussions, and makes it possible to disguise it as a narrative!

The twenty *Homilies,* or Conversations, relate long talks of Clement with Peter about spiritual matters. Both of these books probably go back to an earlier piece of fiction about Clement, written about A.D. 260, but now lost. It clearly made use of the Acts of Peter, and like it had much to say about Simon Magus (originally of Acts 8:9) who played such a part in the Roman scenes in the Acts of Peter. As it is, the Clementines, as *Homilies* and *Recognitions* are called, exhibit heretical and orthodox elements strangely mixed—a fact of which the Catholic Church of the time was doubtless unaware. Letters from Peter and Clement to James of Jerusalem, Jesus' brother, precede the *Homilies,* in order to certify their credibility.

Gregory introduced his account of it with a summary of a later and quite fanciful Egyptian Acts of Andrew and Matthias (or Matthew) among the cannibals, who kept any strangers who fell into their hands for thirty days and then ate them, carefully tagging each one with the date of his arrival, so as to make no mistake. This account in Gregory became the basis of the Anglo-Saxon poem on Andrew (*Andreas*) which some writers have ascribed to Cynewulf, the Old English poet.

The development of Christian fiction, which had produced the five principal books of individual apostolic Acts—Paul, John, Peter, Thomas, Andrew—in the second and third centuries, A.D. 160-260, went on in the generations following into a series of secondary Acts even more grotesque and extreme. There are Acts of Philip, of Peter and Andrew, the Martyrdom of Matthew, and the corpus of such things

entitled the *Apostolic History of Abdias,* who is said to have
been the bishop of Babylon in the sixth or seventh century,
and to have written in Hebrew, in ten books, the Acts of
Peter, Paul, Andrew, James the Great, John, James the Less,
Matthew, Bartholomew, Thomas and Philip. The whole work
seems to be a later imitation and expansion of the collection
of five "primary" Acts already discussed.

So through the centuries Christian imagination went back
again and again to the labors, adventures and hardships of
the apostles, in their far missionary wanderings.

14

APOSTOLIC REVELATIONS

W E HAVE SEEN how Christian piety and devotion, though sometimes badly misdirected, ascribed to the various apostles gospels, acts and epistles until there was hardly an apostle left uncredited with some Christian book or letter, and their leader, Peter, had all three—gospel, Acts and letters. But he even had an apocalypse named for him! Indeed, enough Christian writings were ascribed to Peter and given his name to make a New Testament of Peter—a gospel, an Acts, two letters, the Preaching of Peter and a Revelation of Peter. Of course, none of these compared in importance or value with the one book that really rested on his memories and his preaching, the Gospel of Mark.

While all the rest are not the work of Peter, one of them, the *Revelation of Peter,* is a document of strange interest and history. Believed for centuries to be lost, a considerable fragment of it was found in 1886 in a small parchment manuscript in a tomb near Akhmim in Egypt. Ancient records of its length at 270 to 300 lines showed that this fragment preserved almost half the book. A comparison of this with the so-called Book of Clement, contained in the Ethiopic New Testament, brought to light the whole text of the Apocalypse of Peter, which the Ethiopians had embodied entire in their

165

Book of Clement! This book consisted of a series of revelations supposed to have been communicated to Clement by the Apostle Peter.

These included a description of the punishments of hell and the blessings enjoyed by the saved in heaven. The Book of Clement is extant also in an Arabic version, but the part of it which can be identified as the *Revelation of Peter* was clearly originally written in Greek. Scattered pieces of its text are preserved in Clement of Alexandria, in the Sibylline Oracles, about A.D. 200, in Methodius of Olympus, in the third century, and in Macarius of Magnesia, about A.D. 400. A parchment leaf in Oxford contains twenty-six short lines of the Greek text, and a double leaf from the same manuscript probably of the fourth century, in Vienna, helps toward the recovery of the original Greek text. So on the basis of these various witnesses, Greek, Ethiopic, Arabic, and Greek again, we are in possession of all that this curious "Revelation" had to say.

The leading Christian apocalypse, or revelation, is that of John in the New Testament, but it makes no claim to apostolic origin, and we are seeking to describe the books of the various religious types that make up the New Testament, gospels, acts, epistles, revelations, and see how far Christian literary piety sought to make use of them in building up the figures of the apostles. For in all this writing they were seeking to do honor as they saw it to their historic religious guides, the twelve apostles.

15

THE APOSTOLIC TRADITION

IN 1551, on the Via Tiburtina—the Tivoli road—near Rome and probably near the grave of Hippolytus, a marble statue of him was found which, though much mutilated, contained on the back of his chair a most important list of his principal works, written chiefly between A.D. 200 and 235. One line reads "The Apostolical Tradition About Gifts," probably meaning two works, both lost in 1551. But a series of discoveries beginning in 1848 has brought to light a work of his on the *Apostolic Tradition*. It first came to modern knowledge in a Coptic version, in 1848, under the misleading name of the Egyptian Church Order! The Coptic text of it was brought from Egypt by Tattam and published in 1848. But in 1900 Hauler found in a palimpsest in Verona a Latin text of it, much nearer the original Greek, and subsequent investigations have shown that it is really the long-lost *Apostolic Tradition,* written by Hippolytus of Rome early in the third century, or about A.D. 215, intended in part to set the pope Zephyrinus right about the real rules of the church.

The little book contains information as to how to ordain bishops, presbyters, or elders, and deacons; Hippolytus gives the prayers to be offered on such occasions. It also tells of confessors, widows, virgins, new converts, as well as the crafts Christians must not follow. It deals with baptism and confirmation and just how they are to be celebrated, and gives precise instructions about fasts, prayers, and church observances in general, all in a very definite and practical manner. All this made a small, compact manual, for practical use. Hippolytus was clearly the first churchman to undertake to codify church procedure, indeed he is said to have complained of the bishop Zephyrinus (217) that he was ignorant of the rules of the church.

In the persecution by the emperor Maximin the Thracian, in A.D. 235, Hippolytus and the then Pope Pontius were exiled to Sardinia and there both of them died.

16

THE APOSTOLICAL CONSTITUTIONS

THIS *Apostolic Tradition* of Hippolytus was afterward rewritten and made into the *Apostolical Constitutions,* viii, 4-32, and this again was condensed into the *Constitutions Through Hippolytus.* The original work, the *Apostolic Tradition,* by Hippolytus, was further reflected in the *Canons of Hippolytus,* which have come down to us much altered in Arabic and Ethiopic. Greek was still the language of the church of Rome in the time of Hippolytus, as it had been from the foundation of that church. So his *Apostolic Tradition* has passed from its original Greek into Latin, Coptic, Arabic and Ethiopic in its historical influence. Hippolytus was the last considerable Greek writer of the church of Rome. He shows the use of a New Testament of twenty-two books but not Hebrews, Second Peter, James, Jude or Third John. But he knew James, Jude and Hebrews and is the first Christian writer to reflect Second Peter. He also shows acquaintance with the *Revelation of Peter,* the *Shepherd of Hermas* and the *Acts of Paul.*

In a time of great laxity in Christian life and thought, Hippolytus stands out as a great Puritan in morals, struggling manfully to work out high Christian ideals of moral conduct, as well as doctrine and interpretation. He made a real contribution to Christian progress, although less than a

quarter of all that he wrote has been preserved. His concern
for the *Apostolic Tradition,* as shown by his book, and his
long disagreement with the ruling popes, Zephyrinus and his
successors, until both he and the reigning Pope were hurried off to die in Sardinia, shows his deep concern for preserving the purity of Christian procedures and beliefs as he
understood them. There was indeed a strong faction in the
Roman church that wished to make Hippolytus bishop, that
is pope, to succeed Zephyrinus, but it did not succeed. But
his virtual martyrdom in Sardinia a few years later led the
church to honor his grave with the stately statue to which
we owe the fullest list of his writings that we possess.

17

THE APOSTLES' CREED

~

IT WAS NATURAL for a religion so definitely based on faith and belief to seek a statement of just what it basically believed, especially with the heretical sects of the second century springing up with such zeal, and with such outspoken and able champions. The Apostles' Creed, in one hundred and ten words, is much used in public worship in various denominations, and stands in the Episcopal *Book of Common Prayer* as part of Morning Prayer, page 15, and of Evening Prayer, page 29. The Prayer Book, however, prefixes to it a statement that "any Churches may, instead of the words, 'He descended into hell,' use the words, 'He went into the place of departed spirits,' which are considered as words of the same meaning in the Creed."

The Creed reads:

"I believe in God the Father Almighty, Maker of heaven and earth:

"And in Jesus Christ his only Son our Lord: Who was conceived by the Holy Ghost, Born of the Virgin Mary: Suffered under Pontius Pilate, Was crucified, dead, and buried: He descended into hell; The third day he rose again from the dead: He ascended into heaven, And sitteth on the right hand of God the Father Almighty: From thence he shall come to judge the quick and the dead.

"I believe in the Holy Ghost: The holy Catholic Church; The Communion of Saints: The Forgiveness of sins: The Resurrection of the body: And the Life everlasting. Amen."

The Apostles' Creed originated in Rome, after New Testament times. The New Testament knows only simpler statements of belief, such as the words of Paul and Silas to the jailer at Philippi, "Believe in the Lord Jesus," Acts 16:31. Such more formal statements of belief arose in consequence of conflicts with the sects and their peculiar and distinctive tenets, at Rome in particular in the conflict with Marcion, toward the middle of the second century, and his distinguishing the God of the Old Testament from the God and Father of Jesus. His effort was to cleanse Christianity of all Jewish traits. To do this he began to form a Christian Scripture over against the Jewish Scripture, consisting of the Gospel of Luke, ten letters of Paul and his own book, the *Antitheses* or *Contradictions* showing the points in which the Old Testament was contradicted by Christian conviction. The conflict that ensued made it necessary to define Christian belief in something like a creed, and was one of the forces leading to it.

But Marcionism was but one of the sectarian movements that led the Early Church to seek simple sweeping formulations of its basic and distinctive beliefs. The several Gospels and letters which contributed clauses to it from time to time as it gradually developed occur at once to anyone familiar with the New Testament. Such are a verse in II Cor. 6:18, quoting II Sam. 7:14 "the Lord Almighty." "Maker of heaven and earth" at once recalls Gen. 2:4. "His only Son" recalls John 3:16 and I John 4:9. The traditional line, "He descended into hell," recalls the mission of Enoch to the spirits in prison who had sinned far back in Noah's time, Gen. 6:1-4; Enoch 12:1-6; I Peter 3:19, 20. The allusion in First Peter points unmistakably to the mission of Enoch. The ref-

erence to Resurrection on the third day is in line with the
Gospel accounts. The Ascension accords with Acts 1:9; the
sitting at the right hand of God reflects Ps. 110:1, as well as
Acts 2:33; 5:31, 7:55, 56; Rom. 8:34, etc.

Coming to the third and final paragraph: While the Holy
Spirit is spoken of once in The Psalms, 51:11, and twice in
Isaiah, 63:10, 11, in the King James Version of the Old
Testament the expression "Holy Ghost" does not occur. But
in the New Testament it is used fully seventy times, thirty-
eight of them in the Acts, so much so indeed that it has some-
times been called the Gospel of the Holy Spirit. It is often
used in Paul—Romans, First and Second Corinthians and
Second Thessalonians, as well as in Second Timothy and
Titus. It is used also in Hebrews, First and Second Peter,
First John and Jude. It occurs in the English New Testament
as far back as Wyclif, in 1382.

The Catholic Church is not a Biblical expression, in Greek
or in English. It occurs first in Christian literature, as far as
my observation goes, in Ignatius' letter to the Smyrnaeans,
8:2, written about A.D. 110-117, where I would translate "the
universal church." It is used also four times in the *Martyrdom of Polycarp*, written probably in A.D. 156.

"The Communion of Saints" is an expression not found in
the New Testament, the Apostolic Fathers, or the early
apologists. It anciently meant the spiritual fellowship of believers, which was extended to those who had departed this
life, with whom sometimes a very real companionship and
understanding were felt.

"The Forgiveness of sins" is mentioned in Micah 1:4, and
repeatedly in the New Testament (eleven times in all),
especially in Luke-Acts. (In Eph. 1:7, the Greek reads, "forgiveness of transgressions.") Of course, it is deeply rooted
in the teaching of Jesus, "Forgive, and ye shall be forgiven,"
Luke 6:37, and in the Lord's Prayer, "Forgive us our debts,

as we have forgiven our debtors," Matt. 6:12, or more explicitly, "For if you forgive others," 6:14. The forgiveness of sins is spoken of seventeen times in all in Matthew, Mark and Luke. The phrase appears specifically once in Matthew, 26:28, once in Mark, three times in Luke, and five times in the Acts.

"And the Life everlasting"; the phrase appears in John 12:50; Gal. 6:8, and I Tim. 1:16.

It at once appears that the most of the clauses in the Creed go back to the New Testament, and even to Jesus and the apostles. At a few points, however, in seeking to keep abreast of living problems in the religious life, what was then a more modern phraseology or even doctrine was adopted. Its earliest form, in use at Rome is said by modern scholars to have read simply, "I believe in God the Father Almighty, and in Christ Jesus his Son our Lord, and in holy Spirit, holy Church, and resurrection of the flesh." (So Dr. C. H. Moehlman.) Ancient as its several clauses are, "the traditional text can hardly be traced beyond the sixth century, and the word body, of the eleventh affirmation dates from A.D. 1543." Yet in our earliest discussion of personal resurrection, in First Corinthians, the doctrine of the spiritual body, 15:44, is already presented; I have translated this clause, "It is a spiritual body that is raised."

At whatever dates this or that clause in the great Creed reached its present form, what was steadily aimed at was a statement of doctrine that should, for its generation, be faithful to and in accord with the gospel as it was preached by the apostles. It was always, in aim and intention, the Apostles' Creed.

INDEX